Modeling
AIRLINERS

AARON SKINNER

KALMBACH BOOKS

Kalmbach Books
21027 Crossroads Circle
Waukesha, Wisconsin 53186
www.Kalmbach.com/Books

Published in 2013

17 16 15 14 13   1 2 3 4 5

Manufactured in United States of America

ISBN: 978-0-89024-844-7
EISBN: 978-0-89024-922-2

Editor: Randy Rehberg
Art Director: Tom Ford

All photos by the author or Kalmbach Books unless credited otherwise. On the cover: Aaron filled the
windows, doors, and windshield and improved the tail shape of Airfix's 1/144 scale Airbus A300B. He applied
Hawkeye Models Australia decals to mark the aircraft with Air Niugini's bird of paradise logo from the 1980s.

Dedication
I dedicate this book to my mother, Gail, whose encouragement turned my modeling into a passion, and to
my father, Jim, who gave me an appreciation for airliners and other things with wings.

Publisher's Cataloging-In-Publication Data

Skinner, Aaron.   Modeling airliners / Aaron Skinner.

   p. : ill. (chiefly col.) ; cm. -- (FineScale modeler books) -- (Scale modeler's how-to guide)

   Issued also as an ebook.
   ISBN: 978-0-89024-844-7

   1. Airplanes--Models--Design and construction--Handbooks, manuals, etc. 2. Models and modelmaking-
-Handbooks, manuals, etc. I. Title. II. Title: Airliners III. Series: FineScale modeler books.
TL770 .S55 2013
629.133/134/0423

Contents

Building airliners is fun

build a lot of models of a lot of different subjects—1/48 scale Australian and British military aircraft, 1/35 scale armor (modern and anything Russian), 1/24 scale trucks, and science fiction— but for as long as I can remember, I've wanted to build airliners.

The Story of Three Pioneer Airliners of the Postwar Era

Part of my attraction to model airliners is my love of flying; even today, when air travel seems more like a trial to be survived, I still love to fly. The thrill of takeoff as the engines rev and the overhead bins rattle, the view from 35,000 feet (I always book a window seat), the grind of the flaps extending, and the thump of the main wheels touching down have lost no romance for me. Just being around airports is exciting to me—ask my ever-patient wife, Beth, how I always find an excuse to drive by an airport. In part, I blame my dad for my fascination.

When I was growing up, he and I spent many weekends and school holidays watching the traffic coming and going at Eagle Farm Airport in Brisbane, Australia.

While the focus of my early modeling was 1/72 scale World War II aircraft, I kept trying to build airliners, with varying degrees of success. Most of my early attempts fell short because gloss white and natural-metal finishes are a challenge at the best of times, let alone by hand-brushing. But those frustrations didn't stop me from continuing to build.

Why build airliners?

Put simply, I build airliners because I love the subject. Commercial aircraft are colorful. Airlines use their aircraft as flying billboards, so liveries tend to be bright, bold, and eye-catching.

And talk about variety. Boeing has built more than 7,000 737s since the family was introduced in the late 1960s. Airbus has built more than 5,000 aircraft in the A320 family, including the A318, A319, and A321, since the 1980s. That means you can build hundreds of each and never repeat a

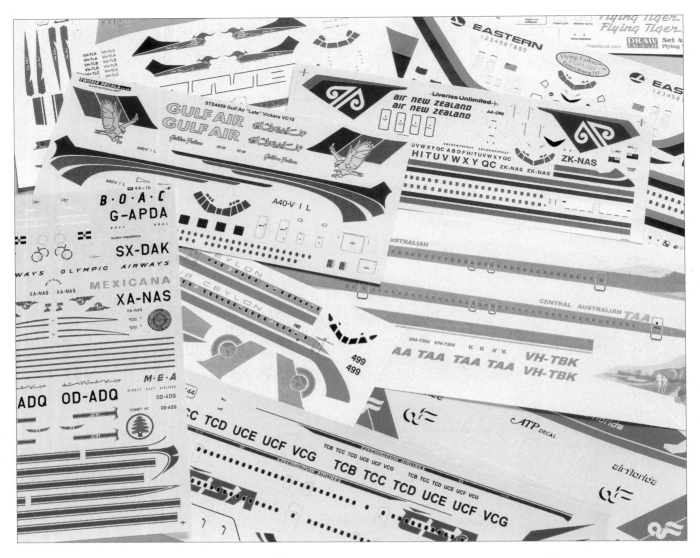

livery. It's the equivalent of modelers who set out to build whole fleets of Messerschmitt Bf 109s or P-51 Mustangs.

Speaking of variety, adding colorful airliners to a shelf of matte gray or green aircraft can provide a nice change of pace.

There's no better time
With the recent growth in the number of new kits being produced, modelers have an ever-increasing selection of airliners and materials to choose from. Old mainstream players like Airfix, Revell, and Hasegawa have been joined by newcomers like Zvezda and Minicraft in producing state-of-the-art, injection-molded kits of modern and classic airliners. Other companies, such as Roden and ICM, have added airliners to their catalogs.

Short-run and independent companies—AZ Model, F-RSIN, Skyline, Amodel—have added injection-molded

kits to the mix. And a whole host of manufacturers, including Authentic Airliners, BraZ Models, and Welsh, use materials such as resin and vacuum-formed plastic to create airliners.

What about some color?
All of those kits are useless without markings. Most kits come with at least one livery, but airline modelers live and die by aftermarket decals. And they haven't been disappointed. The advent of new printing technologies has created an explosion of decal makers. A quick internet search pops up names like Draw Decal, Boa, Hawkeye Models Australia, Vintage Flyer, Flying Colors, and F-DCAL, to name just a few. This means lots of options. And lots of temptation: I'm drawn to attractive airline decals like a moth to a light, which means I have more decals than I have kits to put them on.

What to build
So you've decided to build an airliner, but you aren't sure what to build. Some people build aircraft they've traveled on. I know several current and former airline pilots who built aircraft they crewed.

I also know guys whose intention it is to model every aircraft type flown by a particular airline or to build each version of an airliner, such as the 737-100 through -900.

The theme of my collection is, well, squishy. Having grown up in Australia, I have built several of the aircraft and airlines I saw as a kid: Ansett, Trans-Australia Airlines (later Australian), Qantas, and East-West.

Then there's my intention to model the airliners I've traveled on—Delta L-1011, Kuwait Boeing 777, Continental DC-10, Aer Lingus 737, and Virgin Atlantic A340—and the ones I'll build because the livery looks cool (Braniff) or the decals were too hard to resist (Gulf Air VC-10). Did I mention that I like decals? (Hi. My name is Aaron Skinner and I have a problem …)

A question of scale

An important consideration when building is the scale of the replica. Bigger usually means more detail, but that may not always be the best choice for airliners.

The most common scales for commercial aircraft are 1/144 and 1/200 scales. I prefer 1/144 scale because there are just more subjects available. The major players—Revell, Zvezda, Airfix, Minicraft—as well as many of the smaller manufacturers focus on it. At 1/144 scale, 10 feet on the real aircraft is .067" (1 meter equals 6.9mm). This means a 747-200 would scale out to 19⅓" long with a wingspan of 16⅓". That's a good-sized model. Hasegawa is the main proponent of 1/200 scale and their kits offer a nice compromise—a 747 is less than 14" long.

Other airliner scales include 1/125, 1/100, 1/96, 1/72, and 1/48. I have a few 1/72 scale airliners in my collection, mostly smaller commuter types, such as the Britten-Norman Islander, but I prefer to stick with one scale for consistency in my collection.

Inspiration and information

Want ideas on what to build? Drive to your local airport and see what's on the apron. Just be aware of local laws about stopping on roads around airports. Current security restrictions limit access to many areas, but some airports have places where aircraft watchers can park and take photos.

If you can't actually get to an airport, any airport in the world can come to you via the Internet. In the past, spotters traded and sold slides and prints. Websites have taken their place. The biggest, www.airliners.net, features over 1 million photos, and has a search engine that allows viewers to find aircraft by type, airline, airport, and date. You can even search individual registrations, which is useful if you have decals for a particular airliner. It's a great site for just wandering around and finding airlines and aircraft you may not have been aware of before. Other photo websites such as jetphotos.com may offer images not available elsewhere.

While you are online, check out airline websites, sometimes a good source for photos and information. Manufacturers like Boeing (boeing.com) and Airbus (www.airbus.com) put a lot information, photos, and diagrams on their sites. (Note that Boeing's site has information about Douglas and McDonnell-Douglas.)

Fan sites devoted to airlines and aircraft also provide a lot of stuff you can't find elsewhere.

For a more traditional approach, many books are available. Some are collections of photos grouped by era, airline, or theme. Others are informational and detail an aircraft type with photos and development and service histories. Publishers include Midland, Specialty Press, and Squadron/Signal.

Don't overlook magazines. *Airliners & Airports Magazine, Airways, Air International, Airline World,* and others regularly feature photos of new airlines and aircraft as well as historical surveys and airline spotlights.

Where to buy kits and things

Well-stocked hobby stores carry a few airliner kits or can order them for you if you ask. Getting aftermarket parts or decals tends to be more difficult, but the Internet makes it easier. There are several good specialty vendors. I use Airline Hobby Supplies (www.airline-hobby.com) and Joy Decals (www.joydecals.com) a lot. Many decal and aftermarket parts makers sell their wares from their own websites. Ebay can be useful for out-of-production items.

Have fun

It may seem like a given to say have fun, but remember modeling is supposed to be fun and relaxing. Sure, it can be frustrating when things don't work the way you expect. Don't be afraid to step away from the workbench for a few minutes or a day. And practice the techniques. It takes time and effort to produce good-looking models, but the skills *can* be learned and developed.

1

Construction

Airliners, especially larger subjects in smaller scales like 1/144 and 1/200 scale, are fairly basic builds. They comprise fuselage halves, wings, horizontal stabilizers, engines, and landing gear. Small-scale airliners rarely have any interior detail, so there's little to do before beginning major construction. But that doesn't mean airliners aren't without challenges. In this chapter, I'll show you how to build injection-molded plastic airliners straight from the box.

1 Sharp knives are important for many things in modeling. Keep extra blades on hand because dull ones can damage parts.

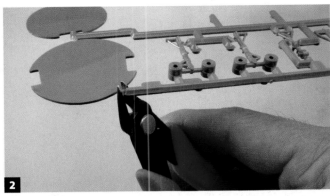

2 Sprue cutters work best for removing parts from the sprue because the flat sides of the blades produce a clean cut.

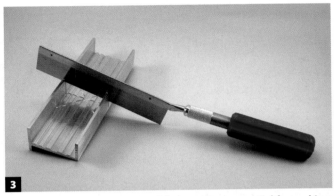

3 Razor saws have a fine cutting blade and are essential for making clean cuts or removing small parts from sprues. A miter box is handy for making straight incisions.

4 Make sure you have several adhesives at the workbench. I use several kinds of solvent cement as well as super glue, epoxy, and white glue.

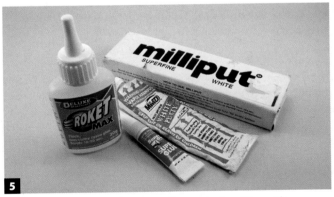

5 Super glue is good for filling small gaps, but putties, either modeling filler or two-part epoxy, are essential tools.

6 Grab a bunch of sandpaper, sanding sticks, and files to clean up parts or smooth seams and surfaces.

Tools

You need a few basic tools to build models. A hobby knife is a must; I recommend one with interchangeable blades, **1**. To cut parts from the sprue, use sprue cutters, or side cutters, **2**. While we're talking cutting tools, pick up a razor saw; I use one to remove delicate parts from the sprue and to scribe lines, **3**. Get a miter box for making square cuts, which is important when sectioning fuselages for conversions.

You'll need various kinds of glue for attaching different parts. Solvent-based glue, like traditional model cement, melts the plastic along seams to effectively weld parts, **4**. Tube glue, the type most of us used as kids, is slow setting and useful for joining large parts. Liquid cement runs along seams. Super glue, sometimes called cyanoacrylate (CA), sets instantly, making attaching certain parts easy. It is available in viscosities from thick to thin

and can also be used to fill small gaps and seams. White glue and 5-minute epoxy come in handy too.

In addition to super glue for filling gaps, pick up some putties, **5**. Model fillers like Squadron and Tamiya are good for small gaps and sand well, but they tend to shrink a little as they dry. I prefer epoxy putties like Milliput and Apoxie Sculpt. They involve mixing two parts together, don't shrink, sand well, and can be

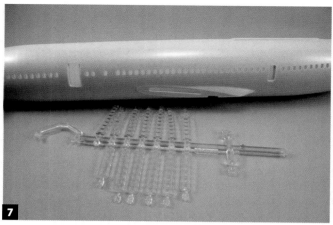

7 Airfix's Airbus A300B includes strips of clear parts that attach from the inside and fill openings in the fuselage to form cabin windows.

8 Strips of masking tape protect the windows on Revell Germany's Constellation as I filled, sanded, and painted the seam.

9 I left the windows out of Zvezda's Sukhoi Superjet, and after painting, filled each with Micro Kristal Kleer applied with wire.

10 Minicraft's MD-80 has a solid fuselage and uses decals rather than openings to represent the cabin windows.

smoothed during application with a wet finger. Both are great for filling windows.

Even the best kits will have parts and seams that need to be cleaned up. Get a set of sanding sticks, with grits from coarse to fine, and sandpaper for body-work and paint preparation, **6**. Metal files can be a bit rough on soft plastic, but a set of rat-tail files are useful for reaming out holes.

Windows

Windshields and cabin windows on air-liner kits are represented in several ways by kit manufacturers. Many older kits and modern Zvezda models include strips of clear plastic windows that are glued into the fuselage, **7**. Some modelers like the realism of open windows, especially the way light can be seen through the cabin. The downside is having to mask the win-dows during painting. If you decide to use them, airbrush the fuselage halves

the final color, white for example, then glue the windows into the fuselage, and join the halves. After cleaning up the join, mask the windows with strips of tape to protect them from overspray while repainting the seam, **8**.

Some models have open windows but no clear parts. For these, and usually even with kits that come with clear cabin win-dows, I build and paint the model and then fill the windows with Micro Kristal Klear, **9**.

Many modern kits have solid molded fuselages relying on decals to reproduce cabin windows, **10**. This eliminates mask-ing. It also addresses another issue: win-dows are sometimes molded in the wrong shape, size, or position.

There are several ways to fill unwanted cabin windows if you prefer decals. If the kit includes clear windows, glue them into the fuselage, **11**. Then fill and blend the windows into the surface with filler putty or super glue, **12**.

If there are no clear parts, clean the inside of the fuselage with alcohol or Testors Plastic Prep. Then, roll out a rope of two-part epoxy putty, place it inside the fuselage, **13**, and push it through the windows, **14**. Flat-ten the putty protrusion slightly to better fill the holes, **15**. Let the putty dry overnight and sand it flush with the fuselage. If you have to do much sanding, protect surround-ing detail with tape, **16**.

Body building

Comedians and some travel writers liken modern air travel to being crammed into a metal tube with hundreds of strangers and hurtling through the sky. The lines are humorous, but the truth is that most airliner fuselages are just that—long cylin-ders with tapers front and back. But build-ing them is not usually as simple as gluing the halves together.

After clipping the parts from the sprue, remove the remnants of the sprue

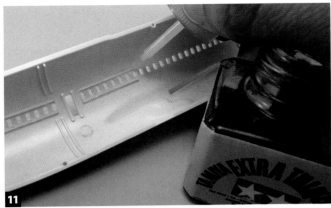

11 I glued the clear windows into the fuselage of Airfix's A300B as the first step to filling the cabin windows.

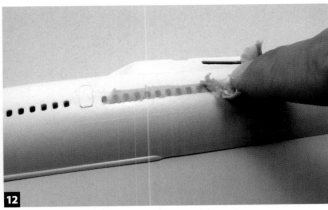

12 I applied Apoxie Sculpt two-part epoxy putty to the A300B's windows from the outside to fill gaps.

13 After cleaning the inside of Zvezda's 767-300, I laid a rope of Apoxie Sculpt across the windows from the inside.

14 I pushed the Apoxie Sculpt through the window openings from the inside so that it protruded 1/16" or so past the surface.

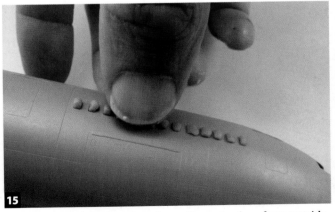

15 Next, I lightly pushed against the putty protrusions from outside, mushrooming them to better fill the windows.

16 Strips of tape protected the surrounding surface as I sanded the putty flush.

attachments with sanding sticks, **17.** Make sure you attach any parts that need to be added inside the fuselage, such as landing gear bays or cockpit parts. If you plan to leave the windows open, paint the interior of the fuselage dark gray or black to hide the lack of detail, **18.**

Many airliners are equipped with tricycle landing gear. This means they need weight or ballast up front to keep the nose wheel on the ground. I use lead fishing sinkers because they are available in several shapes and sizes, and they can be made to fit different spaces.

To install ballast, first gouge the surfaces inside the nose with the tip of a knife, **19.** Then apply 5-minute epoxy or J-B Weld to the surfaces and add the sinkers, **20.** Use enough to keep the nose firmly down but not too much or you risk damaging the landing gear. You can test the weight by taping the major parts together and placing toothpicks in the main landing gear locators.

It's a good idea to test- or dry-fit parts without adhesive to correct problems before committing glue to the seam.

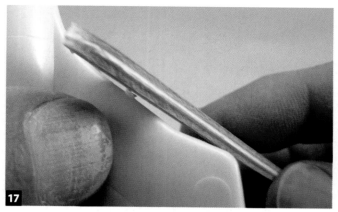

17 When removing sprue stubs from curved surfaces like leading edges, work slowly and watch the angle to prevent damage.

18 I planned to leave the windows of Revell's Airbus A320 open, so I painted the fuselage interior flat black to absorb reflections.

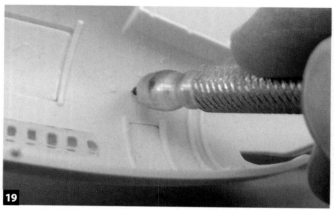

19 Epoxy adhesive sticks better to a rough surface, so I scratched lines inside of the nose of Airfix's Airbus A300B.

20 Fishing sinkers glued inside the nose will keep Revell Germany's 737-800 sitting pretty on all three legs.

21 I held the gap slightly open with a blade, so the glue flowed better. Capillary action pulled it through the gap.

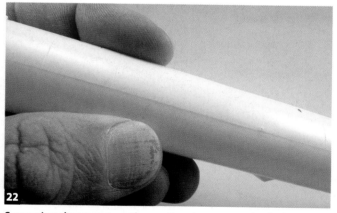

22 Squeezing the parts together as the glue sets pushed a bead of molten plastic from the gap.

Joining fuselage halves is easy using liquid cement. Hold the parts together and place a brush of adhesive to the seam; capillary action will draw the cement along the gap, **21**. After a few seconds, squeeze the parts together forcing a little molten plastic out of the gap, **22**. The ridge can be trimmed flush with the surface, filling most gaps easily.

Use clamps or rubber bands to hold the parts together as the cement sets, which is especially useful if the fit is less than perfect or if the plastic is warped, **23**.

If the seam is long or the plastic is especially thin, you can reinforce it to minimize the chance it'll split during sanding and handling. Add strips of styrene—.040" is good—at intervals on the inside of the

parts, leaving a portion overhanging, **24**. These strips help align the halves and give more surface area for glue. If the parts don't line up quite right, try clipping off the locating pins and align the parts by hand.

Alternatively, on a kit with a large opening—where the wing and fuselage meet, for example—you can reinforce the seam with 5-minute epoxy. Once the

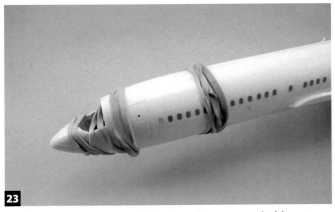

23 Rubber bands provide good all-around pressure to hold parts firmly together as glue dries and to provide solid joins.

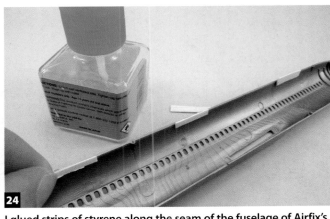

24 I glued strips of styrene along the seam of the fuselage of Airfix's Boeing 727 to help align and reinforce the join.

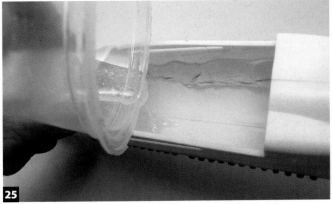

25 I poured epoxy adhesive into the fuselage of Zvezda's Ilyushin Il-86 and let it run around seams to reinforce the large structure.

26 I applied super glue to the seam under the nose of Revell's A320 to fill a gap. A toothpick is great for getting glue in the right spot.

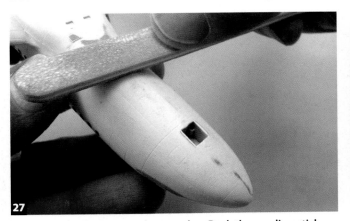

27 Don't wait too long to sand super glue. Rock the sanding stick across the seam to avoid creating flat spots along the fuselage.

28 I spread Deluxe Materials Perfect Plastic Putty along the fuselage of Airfix's 737 to fill minor gaps as well as even out the doors.

liquid cement is dry, pour a little epoxy into the fuselage and then turn it so the glue runs along and coats the inside of the seam, **25**.

If there are separate components, say the nose or tail, add them before going on. Leave off small parts such as antennas until after painting to avoid popping them off the model during handling.

Obliterating seams

Even on the best-fitting kits, such as those from Zvezda, the long seams between fuselage halves rarely just disappear. Some older or short-run kits have part mismatches that create a step along the join. These seams are front and center in the airframe, so it's essential to get rid of them.

To make fine gaps disappear, I prefer super glue. I flow thin super glue along these gaps and apply thicker glue to larger gaps, or steps, **26**. You can speed super glue drying with accelerator, but I use it sparingly since it can damage plastic. As soon as the glue sets, sand it flush with the surface, **27**. Don't wait too long or the glue will be harder than the plastic, making it

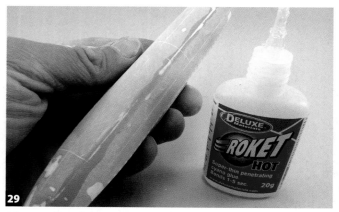

29

After sanding the putty, I covered it with a thin layer of super glue. It sealed the soft putty to make painting and scribing easy.

30

I filled small sinkholes on the engine pylons from Minicraft's 737 with putty and super glue.

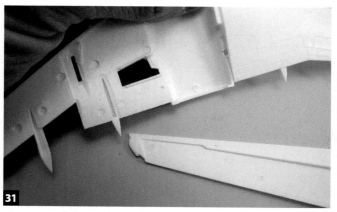

31

The inside of the wings of Revell's A320 are rife with ejector-pin marks, but most of them are inside and will be hidden.

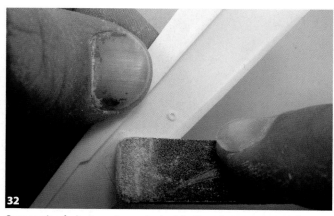

32

Some raised ejector-pin marks inside the wing prevented the halves from fitting together. Sanding solved the problem.

33

Revell's 727 features a windshield frame without clear parts. Note the molded depressions for the cabin windows.

34

The windshield of Airfix's A300B was too big, so I sanded the opening in the fuselage until the clear part fit.

difficult to sand without damaging the surrounding plastic.

For larger gaps, I use filler putty such as Squadron or Tamiya, or two-part epoxy, **28**. Some of these putties have a slightly rough surface, even after sanding. You can fix this by applying a thin film of super glue over the putty and sanding it smooth, **29**.

Pay attention to molding defects like sinkholes and ejector pin marks. The former are small depressions in plastic the occur as the plastic cools and shrinks, **30**. Ejector-pin marks are circular marks left on parts by rods that push part trees from the mold, **31**. These marks can be depressed or raised, and most are on the inside of parts. If they will be visible, fill the holes with putty or super

glue. If they're raised, simply trim and sand them. Occasionally, raised ejector-pin marks will prevent parts from fitting, another reason it pays to dry-fit each assembly, **32**.

Windshields
Kit manufacturers take different approaches to airliner windshields that require slightly different techniques.

14

35 The windshield part of Zvezda's Superjet included a bit of fuselage above the center windows. I blended it with super glue.

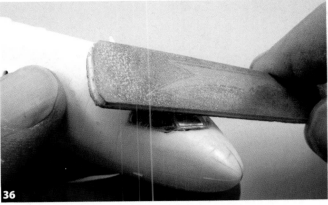

36 After adding super glue to fill a gap around the windshield of Revell's A320, I carefully sanded it to blend it into the nose.

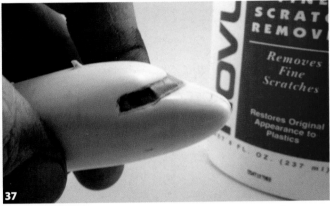

37 Progressively finer sandpaper followed by Novus No. 2 Fine Scratch Remover restored the shine to the Airbus windshield.

38 To prevent the insert from falling in, I glued styrene strips at the rear corners of the windshield opening on Airfix's DC-9 fuselage.

39 It's easy to blend the large windshield insert into the fuselage of Revell's 737-800 without damaging the panes.

40 I positioned pieces of .010" styrene for the frame on an Airfix DC-9. After painting, I filled the panes with Micro Kristal Kleer.

Some mold the frames into the fuselage, **33**. After construction and painting, fill the frames with Microscale Micro Kristal Klear or a similar product.

Others include a piece of clear plastic that fits in an open slot. These can be a little tricky because these parts are thin and can easily be broken if mishandled. Test-fit the part first and file it or the open-

ing so it fits snugly without needing to be forced, **34**. Then glue it into place and mask the frames.

Be prepared to spend extra time and effort filling and sanding the windshield join so that it looks like part of the fuselage rather than a separate piece, **35**.

If the windshield does not fit well, try super gluing it in place and then sand

to blend it into the fuselage, **36**. Rub the clear part with progressively finer grits of sandpaper and polishing cloths to return its clarity, **37**. To avoid pushing the windshield into the fuselage, glue small styrene strips in to the rear corners of the opening, **38**.

Some modern kits, such as those from Minicraft, Revell, and Roden include the

41 Slowly pull the clear part from container of Pledge Future floor polish so the liquid can run off the part without creating bubbles.

42 Drag the edge of the part across a paper towel to wick away excess Future and prevent buildups or runs.

43 You can also use a soft brush to wick excess Future from corners and crevices.

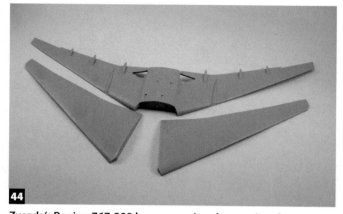

44 Zvezda's Boeing 767-300 has a one-piece lower wing that includes part of the airliner's belly.

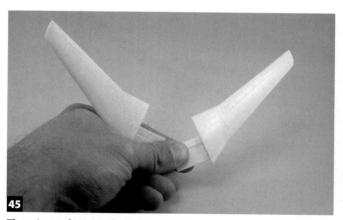

45 The wings of Minicraft's Boeing 737 kits have interlocking tabs that knit together inside the fuselage to set the dihedral.

46 Trailing edges are often way too thick for scale as seen on Minicraft's Boeing 707-320.

windshield as part of a large clear fuselage insert, **39**. This makes it easy to blend the part into the fuselage without damaging the windshield, especially if you mask the frames before sanding.

Instead of trying to fit poor clear parts, you can build a windshield frame. Glue fine styrene strips into the windshield opening using tweezers to locate each piece, **40**. Fill gaps with super glue and sand the area flush. After painting and applying decals, fill the panes with Micro Kristal Klear.

Super glue can fog clear plastic. To protect it, dip clear parts in Pledge Future floor finish. Leave a little of the sprue attached to the clear part to use as a handle, then submerge the part in Future, and remove it slowly, allowing the liquid to run off the part without creating bubbles on the surface, **41**. Blot the part on a paper towel, **42**, or dab excess liquid from the part with a soft brush, **43**. Then hang the part under a cover for at least 24 hours, so it can dry without having dust fall into the finish.

47

I thinned the 707's trailing edges by sanding the inside edges on sandpaper held flat on glass.

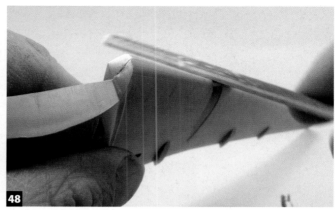

48

I eliminated seams along a 767's leading edge by sanding. Don't sand one place too long to avoid flat spots or unevenness.

49

Seams around the 767's wingbox cross areas that will be hard to hide. I attached and blended the wing before painting.

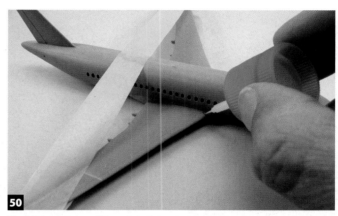

50

I held the wings of Zvezda's Superjet to the fuselage by adding tape under the wingtips and across the body and applied cement.

51

I left the upper wing of Airfix's Handley-Page H.P.42 off the model until after painting and decaling to make rigging easier.

52

Engines on the fuselage or under wings are best treated as subassemblies and painted separately from the airframe.

Wings and horizontal stabilizers

In most kits, wings consist of upper and lower halves, and assembling them is as simple as holding the parts together and applying liquid cement. Some kits have the lower wing molded as a single part including a section of the wingbox, **44**. The advantage of this is that it sets the wing's dihedral and anhedral. Other wings are attached by interlocking tabs that set the angle of the wings, **45**.

When dry-fitting wings, check the trailing edges; they can often be too thick and out of scale, **46**. To thin trailing edges, tape a sheet of medium-grit, wet-dry sandpaper to a sheet of glass and sand the inside surface of the trailing edge, **47**. Even the surface by sanding more of the wing's inner surface, but be careful not to affect the curve of the leading edge.

Also be careful cleaning up seams along leading edges. Sand slowly, checking your progress, and rock the sanding stick to avoid creating flat spots, **48**.

Many horizontal stabilizers are small enough to be a single piece, but be sure you sand off mold seams before painting.

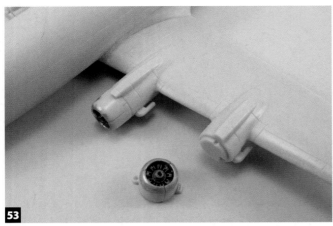

53 I painted and assembled the engines of Minicraft's DC-4 and then glued the cowling to the wings before painting the model.

54 To rescribe a recessed panel line on Minicraft's 727 lost during seam cleanup, I rocked a JLC razor saw across the join.

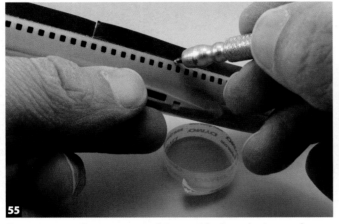

55 Dymo tape makes a great scribing guide. I stuck pieces of it above and below the windows on Airfix's DC-9 to scribe replacements for the kit's raised lines.

56 After painting, applying decals, and adding clear coat, I drew panel lines on Minicraft's 737 with a technical pencil and tape guides (left). You can fix any mistakes with an eraser (right).

Most of the time, it's better to leave the wings and horizontal stabilizer off the fuselage for painting and decaling since these parts can complicate masking and decaling. I make an exception for those kits with a single lower wing. Adding the wing at this stage means it's easy to blend the wingbox seams, **49**. Doing so after painting can be difficult and may require touch-up. To ensure the wing-root seams close, tape the wingtips up as the glue dries, **50**.

There aren't many biplane airliner kits around, but if you have one, you'll want to leave the upper wing separate for painting and decal application, **51**.

Engines

Airliners have different kinds of engines—turbojet, turbofan, turboprop, and piston—and each necessitates different construction approaches. They also require color to be added before construction, and this is best done by hand. Hand-painting is relatively easy. (See Chapter 3 for details.) Once the parts are painted, assemble the engines. On jets, if the hot section can be added later, leave it separate until after painting. In most cases, it's better to leave off engines that are mounted under the wings or on the rear fuselage until after painting and decaling, **52**. For piston-engine aircraft, glue the engine nacelles on and blend the parts as necessary, **53**.

Panel lines

Older kits often have raised panel lines that look unrealistic and should be replaced. Even the engraved panel lines on modern kits get damaged during sanding. The solution is rescribing.

For lost panel lines across seams, I gently stroke a fine razor saw across the gap, **54**. Be careful and work slowly to prevent cutting too deeply.

To replace raised panel lines, I lay Dymo labeling tape along the part. There are specialized scribers available, but I prefer a needle in a pin vise. Gently drag the scriber along the edge of the tape, **55**. Don't press too hard. Don't attempt to scribe the line in a single stroke; instead make several light passes removing just a little plastic each time.

Once the lines are scribed, lightly sand the parts to remove any raised plastic along the scribed lines. If you make a mistake, fill the scratch with super glue and sand it smooth.

FineScale Modeler author Frank Cuden offers an easy alternative to scribing: drawing panel lines with a pencil. Once the model is painted, use tape or a straightedge to guide a fine technical pencil along the surface, **56**.

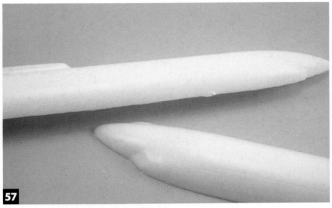

57 AZ Models Tupolev Tu-134 is typical of short-run kits, and the model has rough mating edges.

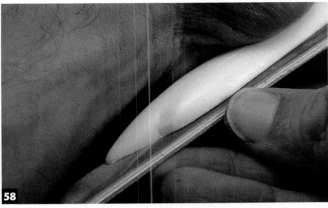

58 I sanded the Tu-134's rough mating surfaces by holding a sanding stick parallel to the part and slowly smoothing it.

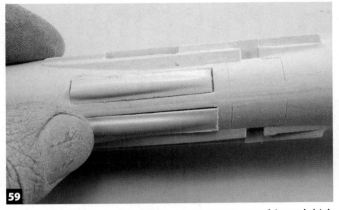

59 The ventral scoops on F-RSIN's Convair 990 were too big and thick to fit their slots. Repeated sanding and fitting made the fit flush.

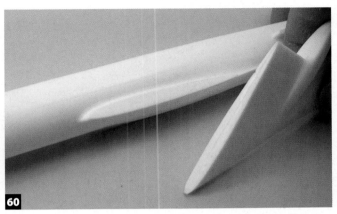

60 The wings of AZ Model's Tu-134 have no tabs or locators. You can attach them as a butt join, but that's inherently weak.

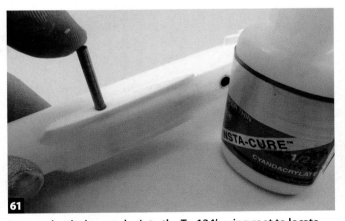

61 I super glued a brass tube into the Tu-134's wing root to locate and anchor the wings.

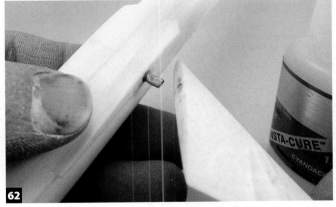

62 After drilling corresponding holes in the wings, I super glued the wing in place.

Short-run kits

Characterized by soft detail, rough molding, and a lack of locators, short-run plastic kits are often the only option if you want to build a particular airliner. They require a little extra work, mostly in preparing parts.

Mating edges are often rough, showing flash or other extra plastic that can interfere with parts fit, **57**. Sanding will even out the edge, **58**. Be prepared to spend extra time dry-fitting and sanding parts, **59**.

The lack of locators isn't a big issue for parts such as fuselages and wings, but it presents more of a hurdle when joining major assemblies such as wings to the fuselage, **60**. To align and reinforce butt joins, drill a perpendicular hole through the part and secure the wire or metal

tubing in it with super glue or epoxy, **61**. Mark and drill corresponding holes in the part to be attached. You can insert a piece of metal tube that is large enough for the wire or tube in the other piece to slide snuggly into. You can then attach the wing by sliding the hole in one part over the protruding rod in the other, producing a solid join, **62**.

2

Painting

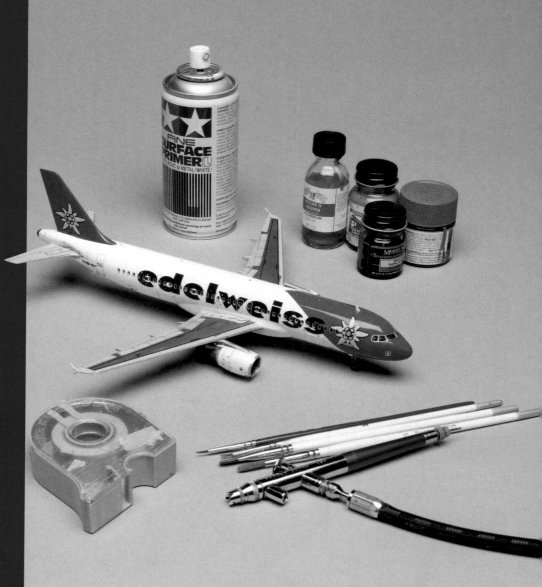

Finish is especially critical when building model airliners because the bright liveries set them apart from their military brethren. But painting them can present a few hurdles: gloss paint (especially white), natural metal, tiny details, and achieving consistent, sharp small-scale masking. In this chapter, I'll work through each of those areas, giving my solutions as well as showing how other modelers tackle them.

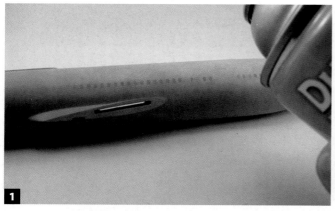

1 Spray cans are widely available and convenient for painting large areas of coverage.

2 You know paint is properly mixed when there are no clumps on the end of the stirring stick.

3 You can add shotgun pellets or BBs to paint bottles to serve as agitators during mixing. Two or three are all that is needed.

4 Clear acrylic lacquer attacked the underlying gray paint on ICM's Tu-144, requiring sanding and retouching to save the model.

Tools

All modelers aim to produce smooth, even coats of paint on their models. This is especially true of small-scale models; a slight ridge of paint left by a brush on a 1/144 scale fuselage would be equivalent to a 1" step on the real thing.

Smooth paint jobs are achievable via hand-brushing, but they are easier to do with spray cans and airbrushes.

Spray paint is convenient and easy to use, but subtlety is not its hallmark, **1**. Spray cans have two speeds—on and off—and they produce a huge volume of paint from the nozzle. This is good for large areas like fuselages, but not great for getting enough paint in tight spots, such as wing roots, without flooding surrounding areas.

Airbrushes are ideal for giving the smooth results of spray paint with the ability to control all the variables. An airbrush is one of the best investments you can make to further your modeling, no matter what you build.

Paint

A trip to a hobby or craft store reveals the wide variety of paint brands and types available to modelers. There are three basic types: enamel, acrylic, and lacquer. Good results can be achieved with any of them, but application methods differ. I use all three depending on the model and the colors I need. I recommend using what you feel comfortable with and the best way to become comfortable is through practice.

As paint settles, it separates into its parts and needs to be thoroughly mixed to apply correctly. Most paint manufacturers recommend stirring the paint until no solid material remains at the bottom of the bottle or tin. I usually start by stirring and then shake the bottle thoroughly until the paint's consistency is even, **2**. Adding a couple of BBs or small metal nuts to the bottle to serve as agitators is a great way to improve paint mixing, **3**.

I tend to stick with paints designed for modeling, although I have used household, craft, and automotive spray paint.

When using a new paint type or brand, test it first on scrap plastic. Some paints, like automotive lacquers, are aggressive, or "hot," and can damage or craze the plastic. But be willing to try new things. I know airliner modelers who, in their quest for the perfect color match have used odd paints and even nail polish.

Be mindful of compatibility when using different paints. As a rule, don't apply lacquers over enamels or acrylics, and don't use enamels over acrylics. More aggressive paints tend to attack the underlying paint and can ruin the finish, **4**.

Finding the right color

Getting exact paint matches can be a challenge. Many kit instructions call for generic colors like green or blue, but a glance at any paint rack shows that there are many greens and blues. Even when the instructions indicate a specific paint, it may be the closest match within a given brand. Aftermarket decal sheets, often designed by airliner enthusiasts, do

PAINT ADVANTAGES AND DISADVANTAGES

ENAMEL

Pros:
• Different brands thin and apply similarly
• Slower drying time helps paint level
• Adheres well to most surfaces

Cons:
• Smelly
• Slow drying time means longer waiting time between coats

ACRYLIC

Pros:
• Many new brands available
• Less obnoxious
• Fast drying time

Cons:
• Different brands behave and apply differently especially when airbrushed
• Fast drying means more dip blockages from drying paint
• Requires more surface prep

LACQUER

Pros:
• Solvent-based
• Fast drying
• Thin coats

Cons:
• Smelly
• Can attack plastic so it's best to prime

---

a good job of pointing out matches or close approximations.

When I'm not sure, I check online to see if anyone has built the same subject and what paint they recommend. Some hobby paint manufacturers make one or two airline specific colors—Revell Germany has Lufthansa blue and yellow. Xtracolor, from Hannants in the United Kingdom, has a large selection of livery colors.

One group of colors may cause more problems for newcomers: the gray used on wings and horizontal stabilizers on many modern jetliners. On Boeing airframes, the color is referred to as Boeing Gray, BAC Gray, and sometimes 707 Gray. Opinions differ about the actual shade of gray used. Xtracolor has a couple of specific options in its range, but many modelers agree that Testors Model Master Canadian Voodoo gray (No. 2035) is a close match. That's what I use. I've also seen British aircraft gray and even Tamiya

insignia white spray paint used. Airbus and McDonnell-Douglas use similar grays.

Surface preparation
It's important to clean the model after construction and between sanding steps to remove oils left by manufacturing and fingers as well as any sanding residue. Paint, especially acrylic, adheres better to a clean, dust-free surface.

I start by washing the model in luke-warm water with a few drops of dish soap added, **5.** Put the model aside to dry; you want to make sure there's no moisture hidden inside wing openings or landing gear bays before painting. Then I swab the model with Testors (formerly Polly S) Plastic Prep, a general-purpose cleansing agent, or isopropyl alcohol, **6.**

Primers and priming
Some modelers skip priming, but I think it is an essential first step in achieving per-

fect paint. Primer provides a uniform surface for subsequent layers of paint, helps seal underlying materials and mask odd colors, and reveals surface blemishes, such as unfilled gaps and scratches that weren't apparent on bare plastic.

So what makes primer different from paint? Most importantly, primer is thicker than paint, so it fills minor scratches and pinholes. It is also sturdier than paint, so it will adhere to the surface—some aggressive primers will lightly etch the surface—and promote the adhesion of subsequent layers.

There are several kinds of primer available; some are designed for models while others are designed for furniture or auto painting, **7.** They come in various colors. White and light gray are the most common colors, but dark gray, black, and red oxide are also available. Most primers come in spray cans, but they can also be applied with an airbrush. The color or type of primer you use should be determined

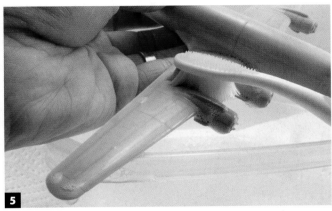

5 I used an old toothbrush to gently scrub Minicraft's DC-4 and remove sanding residue from panel lines.

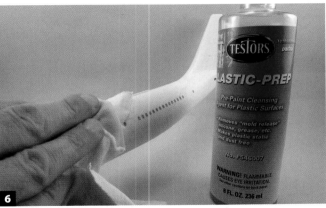

6 Testors Plastic Prep removes oil and reduces static and dust. I applied it to Airfix's Airbus A300B and let the model air-dry.

7 Primers can be sprayed, hand-brushed, or airbrushed. Choose a primer that is compatible with the paint you are going to use.

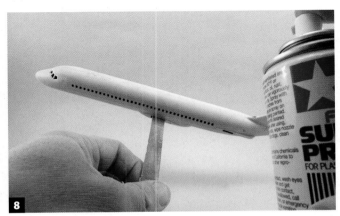

8 When spray-painting, hold the nozzle 6"–8" from the surface and keep it moving to prevent excess paint buildup.

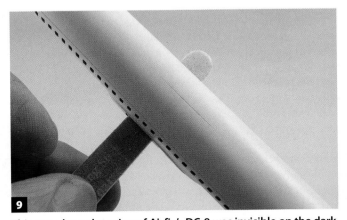

9 This gap along the spine of Airfix's DC-9 was invisible on the dark silver plastic fuselage, but it's obvious after a coat of primer.

10 I filled this scratch, left when a saw slipped on the DC-9, with a little super glue and sanded it smooth.

by the model's raw materials and the colors to be applied over it.

Using a spray can

I usually prime with a spray can. Most airliners are comprised of long thin components that are easy to paint with a spray can.

The most important thing to remember about painting with a spray can is to keep the can moving. Start and end each pass off the model, and don't change directions over the surface, **8**. Spray cans produce large amounts of paint, and any hesitation can create runs. If you get too much paint on the model and see runs or pools, resist the temptation to wipe the excess off the surface. Inspect the area after the paint dries; chances are the paint

will shrink as it dries and conform to the surface. If doesn't, sand the paint and touch it up if necessary.

Applying primer

These instructions apply whether you use a spray can or an airbrush. Spray a smooth layer of primer in several light applications and then inspect the surface. No matter

11 Primer revealed gaps around the windshield on this Zvezda 767. I filled them with super glue and sanded for a clean finish.

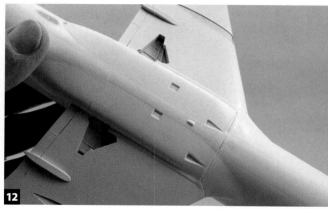

12 One-piece lower wings are great for establishing dihedral, but they can leave gaps under the wingbox. You can fill them with super glue.

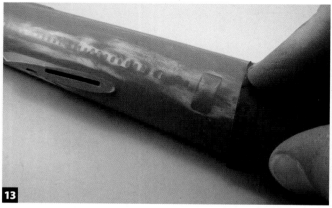

13 After filling gaps on an Airfix A300, I smoothed the fuselage with sandpaper. Note the outlines of the filled door and windows.

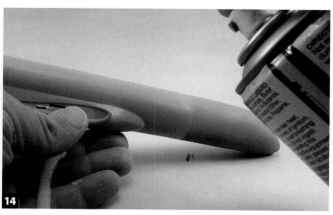

14 After grafting BraZ's resin nose on Minicraft's plastic 757 fuselage, I sprayed Tamiya gray so the color difference wouldn't be obvious.

how well I check seams on a model, the primer always reveals a couple of spots that need a little filler, **9**. They show up better under light gray or white primer.

I fill small gaps with super glue a section at a time. I prefer medium viscosity super glue applied with a toothpick or dental probe. I don't use accelerator because it can be messy, and it will craze the glue. Instead, I dab the glue bubble with a corner of paper towel or a cotton swab to remove most of the excess before it dries. Once the glue is dry to the touch, I sand it flush with the surrounding surface and then move to the next section, **10**. Check and fill around windshields, wing fences, and wing roots while you're at it, **11** and **12**.

Finally, lightly sand the entire model with fine sandpaper—600 or 1000 grit—to even out the surface, **13**. For heavy work, try wet-sanding. Water washes grit and dust away from the surface, which minimizes damage to the surface caused

by debris trapped between the sandpaper and the plastic. It also prevents dust from clogging the grit, so the sandpaper lasts longer. You can either hold the model under a slow-flowing faucet or hold it over a small container filled with water. Add a few drops of dish soap to the water to lubricate the sanding.

Apply another coat of primer to check the seams again, make more corrections if necessary, and repeat until you are satisfied that the surface is perfect.

Primer is also great for covering color changes caused by disparate materials used during construction, such as fillers, resin, or metal, to provide a uniform surface for white or metallic finishes, **14**.

This may seem like a lot of work, but the results are worth it; there just aren't any shortcuts if you want a nice paint job, especially because most airliners feature white and natural metal, which are unforgiving finishes that reveal even the smallest surface imperfections.

Gloss white

No matter what kind of commercial aircraft you are modeling, chances are you will have to paint gloss white at some point. This may be the single hardest part of completing an airliner.

White is a tough color to paint at any time. Add to it the desire to create a smooth gloss finish, and many modelers have run screaming from the workbench. Truth is, a gloss white finish is rarely achieved easily, but it isn't impossible. All it takes is practice.

There are several methods you can use. I recommend experimenting with different techniques until you are comfortable with one in achieving the results you want.

My favorite method relies on the fact that it's easier to achieve a smooth finish with flat white. Start by spraying flat white over the model—Tamiya fine white primer is a great option. Apply light coats until you have an even layer over the fuselage, **15**. Unlike gloss, flat paint is less likely to

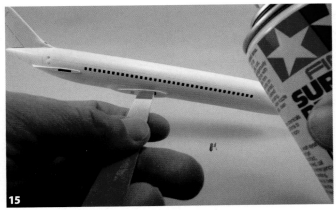

15 I start most white finishes with Tamiya white primer; it goes on easily and produces a crisp, clean white.

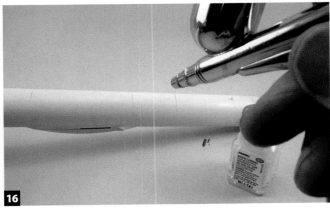

16 I mixed Testors old-school gloss white enamel with lacquer thinner and airbrushed the Minicraft's MD-80 body.

17 Without cleaning the airbrush, I added clean lacquer thinner to the empty reservoir. The result is white-tinted thinner.

18 Spray the thinner mix onto the still-wet paint on the body. You want to mist the paint over the surface rather than flooding it on.

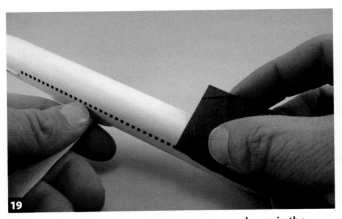

19 Light sanding between coats removes any roughness in the finish as well as any dust or debris that settled in the paint.

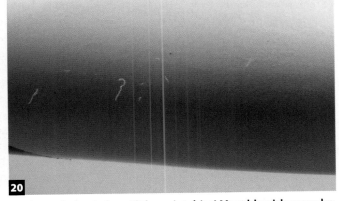

20 Don't touch that hair until the paint dries! Most blemishes can be removed with one or two swipes of 2000-grit sandpaper.

pull away from corners and edges as it dries.

Here's a technique favored by *FSM* author Frank Cuden: first, airbrush the model with Testors square-bottle gloss white enamel mixed with lacquer thinner, **16**. Pour out any leftover paint from the reservoir but don't clean the airbrush. Instead, add a little clear lacquer thin-

ner to the reservoir, **17**, and mist it over the still-wet paint, **18**. This method takes practice, but if everything works, the thinner will cause the paint to blush and then level glass-smooth as it dries.

I let acrylic paint dry for at least a day before continuing; enamels set for as much as a week. Once it's dry, I lightly sand the paint to remove any dust particles or

roughness in the paint, **19**. No matter how careful I am, and how quickly I get a model under cover to dry, a speck of dust or fluff always ends up on the surface. Don't be tempted to pick it out or brush it off during painting; chances are, all you'll end up doing is damaging the paint, **20**.

Be patient and wait for the paint to dry. You'll be surprised at how easy it is

21

I used Mr. Hobby Mr. Super Clear gloss on Airfix's DC-9. After three coats, it produced a mirror-like shine.

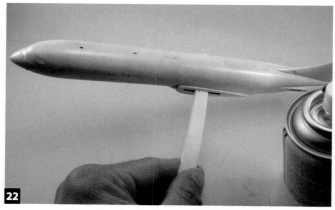

22

Start gloss with a mist coat—some primer should be visible—which gives subsequent layers something to hang on to.

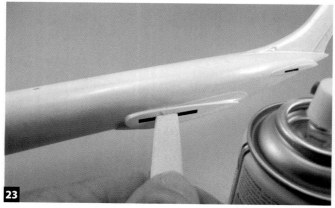

23

The next coat should cover the surface, but it will be a little rough. The finish at this point may resemble an orange peel.

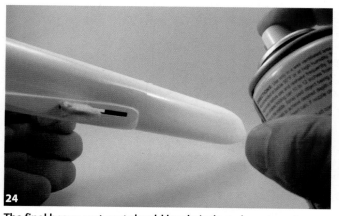

24

The final heavy, wet coat should level nicely and create a gloss finish. Be careful not to apply too much paint.

to remove these kinds of blemishes. It usually takes just a few light passes with fine sandpaper—enough to smooth the surface but not enough to go through the paint.

Next comes a layer of either gloss white or clear applied in light coats, **21**. For a great gloss finish from an airbrush or spray can, start by applying a mist coat over the surface, **22**. Wait a few minutes and then apply a second, heavier coat. This coat should cover the surface, but the layer will not be uniform, and the surface may look a little rough, **23**. Finally, after a few minutes, apply a solid wet coat over the surface. Done right, the paint should create nearly perfect reflections, **24**.

Be careful: there's a fine line between just the right amount of paint and too much paint, **25**.

Other colors

Since Braniff launched the famous flying colors or "jelly bean" scheme in the mid-1960s, color has played a big role

in airliner liveries. Amid the white whale schemes, you can find gold (Southwest Airlines), green (CityBird), and even pink (Helvetic). There's nothing especially different or hard when applying these other colors. The secret is surface preparation.

Most colors achieve full vibrancy when applied over white, so I start with Tamiya white primer. Before applying the next color, I lightly sand the surface with 2000-grit sandpaper to remove any roughness or blemishes.

Next comes the color, applied either with a spray can or airbrush. Start with mist coats and build up the color gradually. The goal is to achieve smooth, even coverage. Avoid the temptation to flood the surface with paint in an attempt to cover it in one session. Not only will that cause runs, but gloss paints tend to pull away from edges and corners as they dry, **26**. Spraying light coats and allowing them to dry a little before the next layer can prevent this haloing effect.

Be aware that underlying colors can affect the appearance of subsequent layers. I mask off those sections before painting the first color, **27**.

Masking

While it's more possible now than ever to paint an airliner fuselage white and complete the livery with decals, sooner or later, you'll need to mask at least the tail or some simple shapes. And in some cases, you may need to do a lot more to complete the scheme. So, let's go to the tape.

The number one method of masking is the old standard: tape. There are many kinds of tape available, and I use most of them when painting airliners. My favorite is Tamiya masking tape because it is thin, flexible, and available in several widths. The downside is it is relatively expensive.

I use Tamiya tape to edge sharp lines and major shapes, **28**. Be sure to burnish the edge to prevent paint bleeding, **29**. Bleeding occurs when paint sneaks past

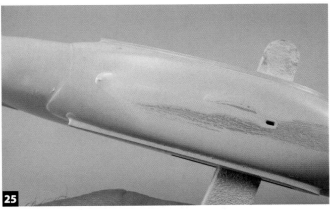

25 I applied too much paint too quickly on Airfix's VC-10, causing it to streak and run under the belly as it dried.

26 Gloss red enamel pulled away from the edges of engraved panels on the tail of Revell Germany's 737-800, creating a halo effect.

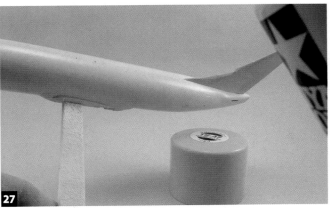

27 I masked the tail of Skyline's 737-300 before painting the fuselage Tamiya chrome yellow. The tail will be painted blue.

28 To mask long, straight lines, I hold one end of a strip of Tamiya tape in place, pull it taut, and then lower it into position.

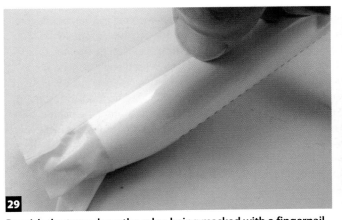

29 Burnish the tape along the edge being masked with a fingernail to prevent paint creeping past and spoiling the finish.

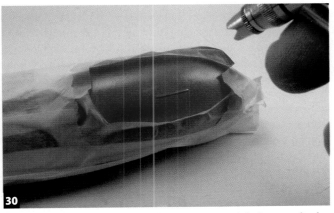

30 I lifted the edge of the tape to feather in a patch being touched up on a Zvezda 767-300.

the mask and flows into places you don't want it to go. I usually run a fingernail along the tape's edge to burnish it. Most airline liveries have hard color demarcations, but if you need a feathered edge, you can either peel up the tape edge slightly or use a paper mask fixed with poster putty or rolled tape, **30**. To produce a neat, soft demarcation, spray either

directly down on the mask edge or from slightly behind, rather than into the mask.

Tamiya tape is also great for masking windshields. You can press a piece into place to cover one or more panes of the window. In most cases, the molded frame should be visible, and it's a simple matter of running the point of a new No. 11 blade along the frame and peeling away the

excess. If the frame is not distinct enough to cut out on the model, use a photocopy of a decal windshield to create a mask, **31**.

You can also trim the tape on the model to fit around pylons or other shapes. Place tape across the panel line or corner and push it in with a fingernail or burnishing tool. Then run the tip of a sharp No. 11 blade along the panel line or

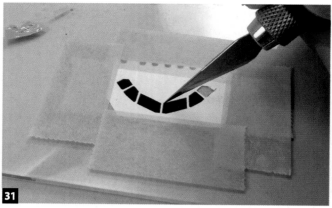

31 I photocopied a decal of an Airbus A320 windshield, secured it over tape, and traced around it with a knife to make a mask.

32 I cut tape around the engine pylon on an Airfix DC-9 in preparation for painting it aluminum.

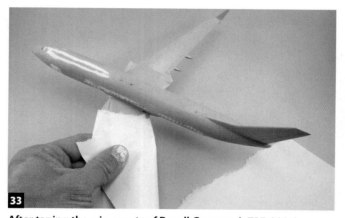

33 After taping the wing roots of Revell Germany's 737-800, I covered the wings with scrap paper held in place with tape.

34 Electrical tape is stretchy enough to go around compound curves and sticky enough to hold a sharp line.

edge, **32**. Do not press hard, you want to cut the tape without damaging the paint.

I also keep a couple of rolls of low-tack masking tape—blue painter's tape and yellow Frog Tape—on hand. It is cheaper than modeling tape, and it's perfect to cover the areas past the edges. I burnish it to the edge tape, but don't press it too hard to the exposed surface so it's less likely to lift paint. For very large areas such as wings, I tape scrap paper behind the edge and wrap it around the object, **33**.

The third type of tape I use is vinyl electrical tape. It is stretchy, so it conforms well to odd shapes and compound curves, **34**. It usually lifts off smooth surfaces with minimum disruption to the underlying paint.

If you are concerned that tape adhesive is too strong and fear damage to the paint, you can reduce the tack by applying the tape to a smooth, clean surface, such as a sheet of glass, and removing it several times.

Other masking tools that are useful include Silly Putty, plastic wrap, Post-it notes, aluminum foil, and even tissue paper. I like Silly Putty for masking voids and spaces like wheel wells. Plastic wrap and aluminum foil are great for masking large areas that need to be protected from overspray, **35**. Post-it notes have straight edges and weak adhesive, so they are useful when masking over metallic and other delicate paints. Tissue paper or paper towels can be pushed into engine intakes and wheel wells.

Begin painting masked areas by airbrushing light coats along the tape edge, **36**. This helps seal the mask, and the light coats prevent paint ridges from forming along the tape. Then, fill the area from the center out, staying away from the masks, **37**.

Odd shapes may need custom masks. Some decal makers provide patterns, or you can use a photocopy of the decals to create a mask, **38**. Lay the pattern over tape and cut it out with a sharp knife.

Remove the tape as soon as possible after painting to minimize paint buildup along the edge of mask. Peel the tape back against itself and pull gently to prevent damaging the paint, **39**. Light sanding should remove any ridge along the edge, but wait until the paint is completely dry, **40**. You can also remove minor bleeding with sanding.

Painting wings

Modern airliner wings are rarely a single color, and they can be challenging to paint not only because of complicated masking but also by having to find the required colors.

Many Boeing and Airbus wings are gray with polished-metal leading edges. Some have Corogard inspar sections, and others have a different shade of gray in these areas. Corogard is an anti-corrosion paint applied to some wings. It looks metallic in some photos and gray in others. Xtracolor's catalog includes Corogard, and I've also used Tamiya metallic gray

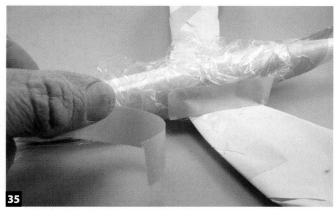

35 I covered the forward fuselage of this 737-800 with plastic wrap in preparation for painting the tail.

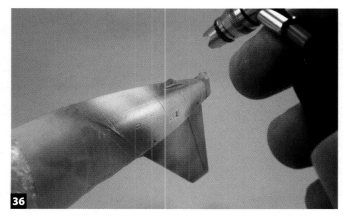

36 Begin painting masked areas by lightly airbrushing along the edge of the mask.

37 Fill the color areas from the center out to minimize paint buildup along the mask edge.

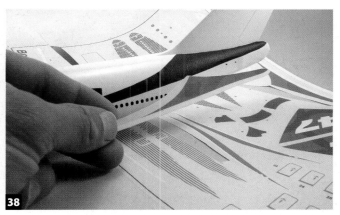

38 I cut copies of the decals for Zvezda's 747-8 and then transferred the shapes to the tape to mask the complex Boeing scheme.

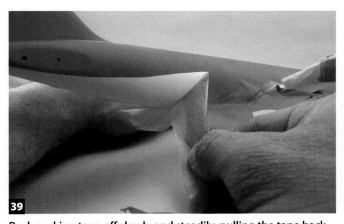

39 Peel masking tape off slowly and steadily, pulling the tape back over itself to help prevent removing any paint.

40 To remove a minor ridge at the edge of the orange paint on an Australian 767, I rubbed it with 2000-grit sandpaper.

and Testors Model Master Metalizer dark anodonic gray on these areas.

I've seen two or three shades of gray with patches of natural metal on MD-80 wings and polished aluminum leading edges.

Undersides are often different from tops. Further complicating the situation is the fact that the pattern can differ from one aircraft to another. Research is impor-

tant in determining the best option for the aircraft being modeled.

Several decal manufacturers make gray or Corogard sections appropriate to specific aircraft types.

Metallics

At one time, most airliners went unpainted. Even today, when liveries cover most of the

airframe, sections like the wing's leading edges and engines have metal areas. This means mastering natural-metal finishes.

There are lots of options, from silver paint to specialty enamels and lacquers to self-adhesive foil. All have their place in airliner modeling.

To paint leading edges, I like Alclad II polished aluminum, **41**. I prefer Floquil old silver

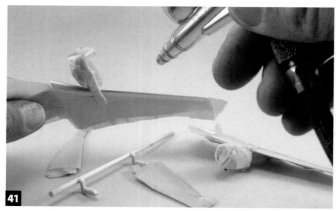

41

Airbrush Alclad II at 12–15 psi and apply it in light coats. I used polished aluminum to paint the leading edges of a Minicraft 737.

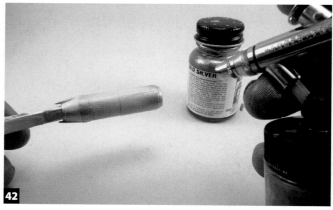

42

Engine intake rings aren't usually as shiny as leading edges, so I paint them with Floquil old silver.

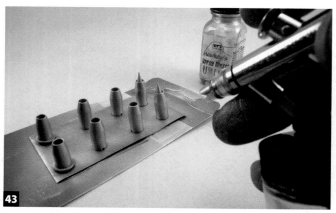

43

I attached the hot sections of 737 engines to a piece of cardboard while airbrushing them Hawkeye's Spray Metal aluminum.

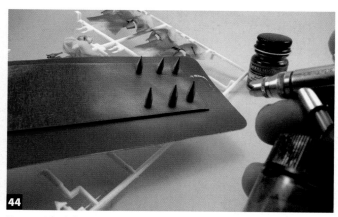

44

Testors Model Master Metalizer burnt metal looks great on exhaust sections. Metalizer must be applied with an airbrush.

45

I airbrushed Minicraft's C-54 with Alclad II Primer and Microfiller to fill and eliminate scratches and small gaps.

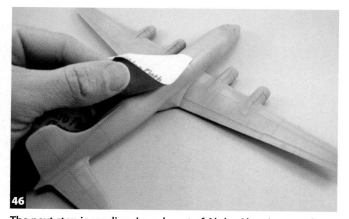

46

The next step is sanding. I used a set of Alpha Abrasives sanding cloths to polish out the primer on the C-54.

enamel for bare-steel jet engine intake rings, **42**. The hot section of an engine usually reveals several metallic shades. You can find a variety of shades from Testors Metalizer, Hawkeye's (formerly SnJ) Spray Metal, and Alclad II, **43**. Metalizer burnt metal is a great option for heat-affected exhausts, **44**.

Metallic finishes starkly reveal every blemish or scratch in the surface, so good surface preparation is absolutely essential. This is even more important when painting an overall natural-metal finish.

After construction, prime the model with Mr. Surfacer or Alclad II Primer and Microfiller, **45**. These thick primers help fill sanding scratches. Fix any problems and then reprime. Once you're satisfied the model is blemish-free, begin sanding the primer with progressively finer grits, **46**. I usually start with 2000 grit and work through 3200, 3600, 4000, 6000, 8000, and 12000. To achieve the best results, it's important not to skip any grits.

Applying metallic finishes over gray produces slightly weathered aluminum, **47**. You can vary the finish by masking panels and airbrushing different shades,

47

I started the finish on the little Douglas with an overall coat of Hawkeye's Spray Metal aluminum.

48

After 48 hours, I masked several panels on the C-54 and then airbrushed Floquil old silver to create variation.

49

To get the most out of Alclad II's high-shine finish, you need a gloss black surface, such as Alclad's base.

50

I sprayed Alclad II airframe aluminum over the lower fuselage of Minicraft's 707 in preparation for Pan Am decals.

48. To create polished bare metal, I airbrush Alclad II gloss black base over the primer and sand it glass smooth, **49**. Then I airbrush Alclad II airframe aluminum, building up the finish through several mist coats, **50**. These lacquers produce a high-shine finish and are pretty sturdy so they hold up well under masking.

Self-adhesive foil can be useful, especially for leading edges. First, cut a piece slightly larger than the area to be covered, **51**. Slip the tip of the knife under a corner and gently peel the foil from the backing. Transfer it to the model and burnish it with a cotton swab, **52**. Run the tip of a fresh (sharp) knife along the engraved panel line and peel off the excess foil.

Decanting spray paint

There are times when a necessary color is only available in a spray can, but delicate work is better served by using an airbrush.

Tape part of a straw or tube over the nozzle of the spray can and secure a piece of kitchen foil or plastic wrap over the mouth of a jar or bottle—an empty, clean paint bottle is a great option. The jar should have a lid that can be closed tightly. Poke the straw through the foil, **53**.

Press the spray can's button and paint will flow through the straw into the jar. Once you have enough, remove the straw and set the jar aside without closing the lid tight. The paint needs to sit for several hours while the propellant boils out, **54**. Then close the lid until you are ready to use the paint. Don't shake the paint until the jar has been opened at least once to release any pressure that may have built up, or you risk being sprayed with paint.

Airbrushing Future

Pledge Future floor polish (from S.C. Johnson) is a clear acrylic coating designed for vinyl flooring that works exceptionally well for modeling. It dries rock hard, is very sturdy, and levels out beautifully. It also doesn't react with enamels, acrylics, or lacquers, and it can be applied with an airbrush or by hand. All it takes is, you guessed it, practice.

Future can be airbrushed straight from the bottle or thinned slightly with 91 percent isopropyl (rubbing) alcohol. I set the pressure at about 20 psi and begin by laying down a few mist coats to wet the surface, **55**. Then I continuously apply slightly heavier layers until the surface looks glassy. Be careful not to apply too much Future in any one spot as you can create runs or drips. If this happens, don't try and fix it by wiping the excess of the surface. Wait until the Future is dry—usually 48 hours—and then check the spot again. More often than not, the blemish will be diminished or eliminated, **56**. If not, lightly sand the area and apply a little more Future.

Other clear coats work—I've had good luck with Tamiya and Gunze Sangyo spray-can clears—but quicker drying times can create rough or orange peel finishes. I recommend trying a couple, find the method you are most comfortable with, and practice until you consistently achieve good results.

51 To cut Bare-Metal self-adhesive foil, score it lightly with a knife, pressing just hard enough to cut the foil but not the backing.

52 After folding the foil around the leading edge of a 737 wing, I burnished it with a cotton swab.

53 Poke a hole with a straw through a piece of foil secured over the mouth of a jar with a rubber band.

54 Bubbles in the primer are propellant boiling out. Let decanted spray paint sit several hours to remove all unnecessary chemicals.

55 Airbrush Future floor polish by misting coats onto the surface to wet it and then add slightly heavier coats to build up the shine.

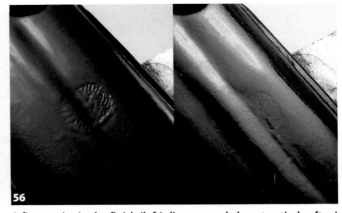

56 A fingerprint in the finish (left) disappeared almost entirely after I let the Future dry for 48 hours (right).

Hand-brushing paint

Small parts like engines and landing gear require hand-painting. Invest in several good-quality paintbrushes; they may cost a bit more, but they will last a long time if cared for. Pour a little paint into a palette reservoir and some thinner into a neighboring reservoir, **57**. You can find inexpensive palettes at art supply stores or even use plastic lids or food containers.

Dip a brush into the thinner and remove most of the liquid by stroking the brush across the lip of the container, **58**. Wetting the bristles helps paint flow and prevents paint from drying in the brush. Then, dip the brush into the paint and draw it against the lip to remove the excess. Apply the paint in smooth, even strokes, **59**. Avoid adding too much at one time and don't drag the brush back over paint already on the model; the surface will have started to dry and show strokes or peel under the brush.

Washes

It can be useful to deepen shadows and recessed details, especially around

57 Always brush paint from a palette or other container rather than directly from the bottle to avoid drying out the paint.

58 Start brush-painting by wetting the bristles with thinner to prevent paint drying in the brush.

59 Apply paint with smooth even strokes, being careful not to apply too much paint and going back over just-painted areas.

60 I flowed a wash of black artist's oil into the engine fan of Zvezda's 767, giving the impression that the blades are separate.

61 The secret of dry-brushing is to remove as much paint as possible from the brush by stroking it across paper before painting.

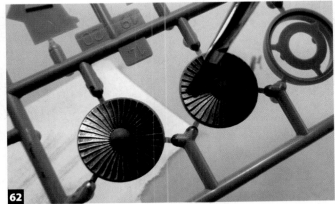

62 Dry-brushing deposits Testors chrome silver on the top edge of the 767 engine fan, further reinforcing the 3D effect.

engines and landing gear with a wash. A wash is very thin paint that settles into grooves and recesses. If you painted the parts with acrylics, use an artist's oil or enamel wash. Apply an acrylic wash over enamels or lacquers.

Mix a drop or two of paint into the thinner. The ratio of paint to thinner affects the density of the wash as well as how well it flows. Touch a brush filled with wash to the part and let the thin paint flow across the surface, **60**. If the effect isn't intense enough, apply a second or third wash; the effect is cumulative.

Dry-brushing

Just as washes deepen shadows, dry-brushing adds highlights. Dip a stiff, flat brush in paint and then repeatedly stroke the brush across a sheet of paper to remove most of the color, **61**.

You'll know you're ready to dry-brush when little or no paint comes off on the paper.

Lightly rake the brush across raised detail, **62**. It should deposit just a little paint across the edges of the part.

3

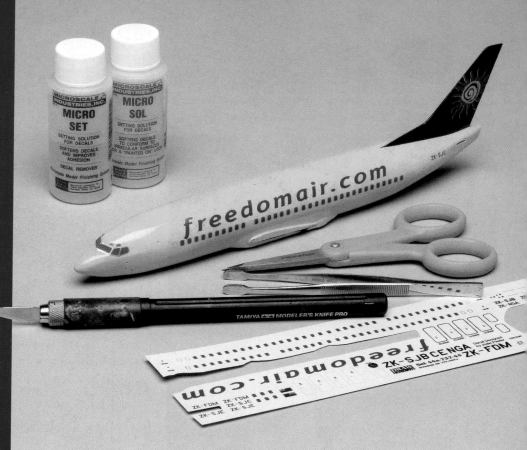

Applying decals

One of my favorite parts of any build is adding the decals. This always seems like the moment when a painted piece of plastic takes on recognizable elements of realism.

1 The TwoSix Decals sheet (at left) features individual clear coat, which can be seen as a glossy outline around each marking. The Draw Decal sheet (at right) is printed with a continuous layer of clear coat.

2 For cutting decals, you can use a sharp hobby knife and a small pair of scissors. Use the scissors only for cutting decals in order to preserve the edge and minimize damage to decals.

3 I have paintbrushes dedicated for decal use. Using the same brushes for both paint and decals can result in flecks of paint on the model. I use toothpicks to move small decals on the model.

4 Decaling is a wet process. Use paper towels and cotton swabs to soak up extra water and to press decals into the surface.

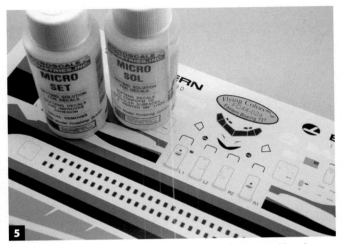

5 I almost always use Microscale Micro Set and Micro Sol but keep other setting solutions on hand for some types of decals.

What are decals?

While modelers occasionally use dry transfers—markings that are applied using pressure—most airline liveries come in the form of water-slide decals. In general, these decals are formed of layers of ink over a water-activated adhesive.

Traditionally, they are screen-printed, but many aftermarket decals are now produced on inkjet, laser, and other small printers. These different production methods require slightly different application.

Decals produced by Microscale and other major manufacturers are screen-printed with clear coat over individual markings. Aftermarket screen-printed decals, such as those from Flightpath and Draw, have a continuous layer of clear coat. This means that each decal must be cut close to the marking. The same is true for laser or inkjet printed decals. If the instructions don't specify whether the sheet has continuous or individual clear coat, examine the sheet closely by holding it at different angles under a light, **1**. You should see a slight difference at the edge of the clear coat. Some sheets don't have clear coat and require an application of decal film before use.

Laser and inkjet printers can't print white, and their decals tend to be a little thin. They often come with separate sheets of white decals produced on an ALPS printer that are applied first to back the livery decals.

Be sure and read the instructions that come with each set of decals, and don't assume that what works with one will work with another.

For example, Draw Decals are printed using a digital silk-screening technique that produces dense colors, but the ink is a little thick and unaffected by setting solutions. Instructions included with each set or those found on a company's website tell you to use hot water to soften the ink during application.

Tools

To remove decals from a sheet, I use a dedicated pair of small, sharp scissors and a hobby knife, **2**.

I keep several brushes solely for decals and setting solutions, and use toothpicks to manipulate decals on the model, **3**. You'll also need paper towels and cotton swabs to remove excess water, **4**. Look for good quality medical swabs that are less likely to shed fibers during application.

Setting solutions are essential in helping decals conform to the surface, **5**. There are several brands, and each is a little different, but they all soften the decals. Some are stronger than others, so it's a good idea to test them on a spare decal before using them on a full sheet.

6 Flightpath's Ansett 737 sheet has continuous clear film. It's important to trim any decal as close as possible. I lightly scored around each marking with a brand new No. 11 blade.

7 Small scissors are easy to maneuver between markings when cutting decals from the sheet. I removed the reference number between the MD-80 eyebrow windows before soaking the decals.

8 I dipped the windshield in a container of warm water for a few seconds, just long enough to saturate the backing paper. Don't leave decals floating in the water.

9 Place decals on a paper towel rather than keeping them in the water. The towel absorbs excess water as the adhesive is activated.

Removing decals from the sheet

It's a good idea to remove as much excess clear coat as possible whether you are using decals with individual sections or with continuous clear coat. Before cutting a marking from a sheet, lightly run a sharp hobby knife around the edge of the marking, **6**. Don't press too hard; you don't want to cut all the way through the backing paper, just through the clear coat. Cutting the decal out of the sheet too close to the marking can damage the edge.

Then, using a sharp scissors or hobby knife, remove the decal along with some of the surrounding paper, **7**. Be careful not to bend or crease the paper or cut through nearby decals.

Wetting the decal

Immerse the decal in warm, not hot, water for a few seconds to activate the adhesive, **8**. Then place it on a paper towel or other absorbent material and let it sit for 30–45 seconds, **9**. Don't leave the decal in the water or let it float off the paper in the container. Sitting too long in the water will dissolve the adhesive and prevent the decal from sticking. Trying to corral a loose decal can be problematic because there's a good chance that it will fold back on itself and be hard to straighten without damaging the marking.

While the decal is on the paper towel, wet the area of the model where the decal will be applied with Microscale Micro Set, **10**. You can also use water, but Micro Set breaks down surface tension and promotes adhesion.

Positioning the decal

Lightly touch the decal with a cotton swab and see if it moves freely on the backing paper. Don't force it, or you risk tearing the thin film. Let the decal sit until it does move.

Use a toothpick to remove excess clear coat from around the marking and discard it, **11**.

Place the edge of the paper on the model near the spot where the decal goes. Hold one end and gently slide the paper away, letting the decal settle onto the model, **12**. Fine-tune the marking's position with a brush, **13**. If the decal doesn't move easily on the model, add a little water. You can gently work a wet brush under the edge of stubborn decals. Manipulate small decals with a wooden toothpick but work gently, **14**. Don't use a knife.

I begin applying decals where positioning is determined by fuselage detail. Windshields are a good starting place because the shape of the fuselage dictates their position. Then, I place the major elements of the livery, **15**. I add stencils last because they are usually painted over the airline's markings.

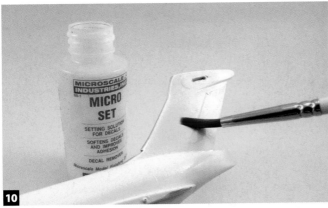

10

While the SAS logo was sitting on a paper towel, I brushed Micro Set on the tail. Micro Set is a mild acetic acid with a wetting agent that prepares the surface and promotes adhesion.

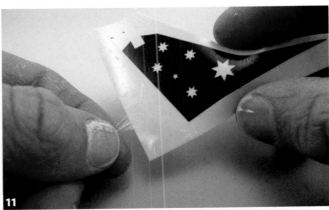

11

I removed the clear coat from around the Ansett tail flag before positioning the decal.

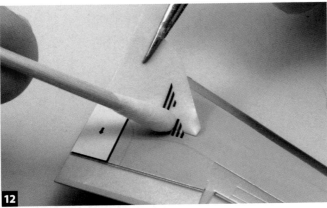

12

Use a brush or toothpick rather than a finger to slide the decal from the paper—decals tend to stick to skin.

13

I used a wet brush to massage the MD-80 windshield into position. Use a little extra water if the decal doesn't move easily.

14

I had to assemble the registration on this Qantas 737-800 from individual letters. A toothpick made fine-tuning each letter's position easy.

15

On this DC-9, I started applying Texas International markings with the tail logo; it's easily located and the rest of the livery naturally aligns with it.

Positioning long decals like cheat lines or windows can prove difficult, so be prepared to spend extra time getting them right.

If the kit doesn't have open windows, use other surface details to help place stripes. Cabin doors are a good place to start. Even if I fill them, I try to leave part of the impression of one or two just for positioning decals.

Check the alignment of long decals by looking down the side of the fuselage, **16**. You can check the position of decals on each side of the fuselage by looking down on it, **17**. You can also check decal posi- tion relative to the centerline with a pair of dividers, **18**. Keep in mind that titles, often positioned relative to doors or other fixtures, may not be directly across from one another, but you should be able to see how far each side's decals are from the fuselage centerline.

16 Looking down the fuselage from the nose or tail is a good way to spot alignment problems on long decals like cabin windows or cheat lines. Small waves are easily spotted from this angle.

17 Looking down on the fuselage of Revell Germany's 737-800 makes it easy to gauge the relative location of titles and windows as well as their alignment relative to the fuselage.

18 Using a pair of dividers, I checked the distance of the decal windows from the centerline of Minicraft's 737. Ensuring both sides are the same distance prevents the airliner from looking lopsided.

19 I blotted excess water from a Scandinavian MD-80 tail with a wad of paper towel. I pressed a section at a time, rather than trying to press the entire decal at once, which is a good way to inadvertently move the decal.

20 To absorb excess water from smaller decals, like the windshield on this MD-80, I rolled a cotton swab across it, pressing lightly.

21 I waited 10 minutes and then brushed Microscale Micro Sol over the cabin window decals on Minicraft's 737-300. Don't brush too hard, so you don't move the decal.

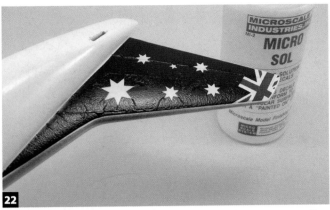

22 Within minutes of Micro Sol being applied, the 737's Ansett tail logo looks unpleasantly wrinkled. Don't panic: it'll be all right.

23 Within a few hours, the Micro Sol dried, leaving the Australian flag on the Ansett 737 looking like it was painted on the model.

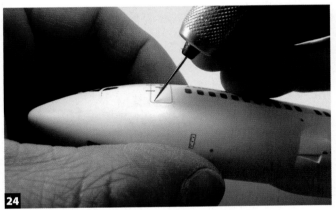

24 I poked holes in air bubbles on the decal and applied Micro Sol.

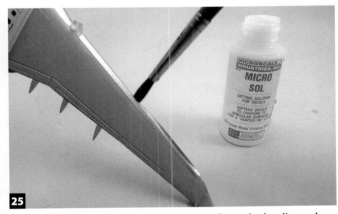

25 It took several application of Micro Sol to force the leading-edge decals on Revell's 737-800 to soften and wrap around the wing.

26 I airbrushed several thin coats of Future to give Minicraft's 737 a uniform shine and to seal the decals.

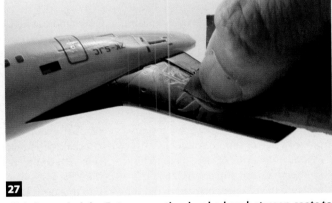

27 I lightly sanded the Future over the decal edges between coats to eliminate any hint of a ridge.

Getting decals to conform

Once a decal is located in the right place, blot it with a paper towel or cotton swab. Apply pressure to the paper towel to force water from under the decal and force the decal into recesses, **19**. Roll cotton swabs over decals, especially those with small markings, to remove any extra water, **20**.

Many decals will settle into the surface as they dry. Others need a little persuasion. If a decal doesn't settle into panel lines, apply a setting solution like Microscale Micro Sol or Walthers Solvaset with a large, soft brush, **21**. Stronger than setting solutions, solvents soften decals causing them to wrinkle, **22**. Don't be tempted to touch the decal and don't blot

it, because it's easy to tear or distort the marking. As it dries, the decal will flatten out and settle into detail, **23**. If you see bubbles in the decal after it dries, poke holes in the decal with a knife or pin and apply a little more solvent, **24**.

Solvents are great for getting decals to go around corners or conform to complex shapes. Get the decal into position, blot

28

I applied white glue to join the wings to Minicraft's 737-300, concentrating the adhesive inside the join.

29

After pushing the wings into place, I removed white glue squeezed out of the join with a cotton swab damp with water.

30

I made a temporary jig to hold the 737's horizontal stabilizer in position as the white glue dried. The final join is strong, and white glue is unlikely to damage paint or decals.

31

When checking the alignment of landing gear, I check from the sides and front to be sure that they are all straight.

away excess water, and then generously apply decal solvent to the marking, softening it until it bends around details, **25**.

After decals

Once the decals dry—I like to leave them for a couple of days—wash the surface with a little water to remove any residue from adhesive or setting solution.

Apply thin layers of clear gloss to tie together the paint and decals, **26**. If the decals are thick, it may be hard to get the edges to disappear. Between coats of clear coat, lightly sand the edges to help even out the surface, **27**. I like the finish to be smooth but not so heavily glossed that it looks like a diecast-metal toy.

Final assembly

Now you can complete the model. Be careful and use glue sparingly when attaching subassembly parts because cleanup can be difficult. White glue is a good option here because it doesn't affect

paint and can be cleaned up with water, **28** and **29**. The downside is that white glue takes several hours to set, so the model must be braced, **30**.

Alignment is critical when attaching landing gear legs so all the wheels touch the ground. If possible, I push them into place and then stand the model on them, checking the position from the front and sides, **31**. Once I'm satisfied with the position, I flow small amounts of super glue into the joins, **32**.

Decal troubleshooting

There are few things in modeling more frustrating than decal problems. When the model is almost finished, the last thing you want is bad decals. Here are a few common problems and how to fix them.

Silvering: This effect makes decals look shiny, as if obscuring the underlying paint. Silvering results from air being trapped between the decal and the surface, and it is usually caused by applying

decals over non-glossy paint. To avoid the problem, always decal over gloss. If the decals are on and refuse to conform to the paint, poke several pinholes in the decal and brush on decal solvent, **33**.

Not sticking: Some decals just refuse to stick. Try painting thin white glue under a troublesome marking, **34**.

Shattered decals: This is just depressing; there's nothing like watching that beautiful decal fall apart, **35**. It happens when the clear film deteriorates and leaves nothing to hold the ink together. There's nothing you can do about the shattered decal, but you can salvage the rest of the sheet by replacing the clear coat. You can brush on Microscale Liquid Decal Film, **36**. Other decal films are available in spray cans, and you can airbrush on Future or other clear coats.

Wrong position: If you discover you've got the decals in the wrong place and need to start from scratch, you can remove the markings with tape, **37**.

32 I added a drop of super glue to the landing gear struts on Minicraft's 737 with a sharpened plastic applicator.

33 The silvering on this decal wasn't obvious until I gloss-coated the model. I poked holes through the clear coat and decal and then brushed on Micro Sol to eliminate the problem.

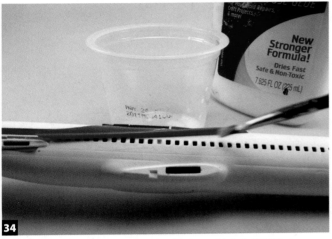

34 The old Microscale decals I applied to turn Airfix's DC-9 into a Hawaiian Air aircraft didn't want to stick. I brushed thin white glue under the edge to encourage them to adhere.

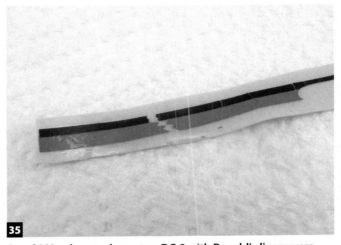

35 Aaagh! My plans to decorate a DC-9 with Republic livery were dashed when the ATP cheat line decal disintegrated after being soaked in water.

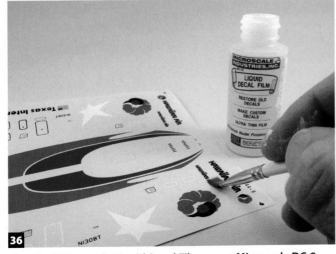

36 I brushed Microscale Liquid Decal Film over a Microscale DC-9 sheet. The film only takes a few minutes to dry and then the decals can be applied normally.

37 After all that work, I discovered I had put Draw Decals SkyExpress markings on too high. I burnished blue painter's tape over the decals. When I peeled it off, the livery came with it.

4

Conversions

Almost all airliner designers have changed their aircraft's capacity over the years. The 103-seat Boeing 737-100 became the 115-seat 737-200 and ultimately the 737-900. The Airbus A320 was stretched to create the A321 and shrunk to create the A318 and A319. Douglas produced some seriously flexible airframes. The DC-8 was stretched more than 37 feet; the initial DC-9 sat 80 passengers in a 104½' fuselage before the airframe underwent seven changes including the 147' MD-80.

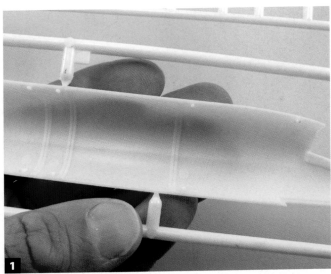

1 Minicraft's beautiful DC-8 kit is molded as the longest member of the family, the Series 61/71. Lines engraved inside the fuselage halves make converting it to one of the shorter versions easy.

2 After determining how much needed to be removed to convert Airfix's DC-9-30 to the short -10, I marked the cuts with masking tape. Note that the lines run along window frames.

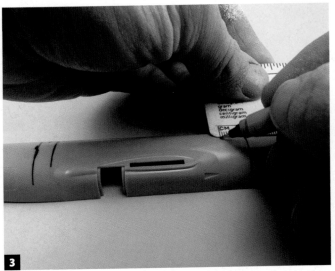

3 Minicraft's 737-300 doesn't have windows, so I measured the cuts with a straightedge to convert it to the 737-500.

4 A miter box and razor saw make quick, clean work of fuselage cuts.

Some changes involve modernizing the airliner's engines and avionics, but in many cases, the changes are reflected in changing fuselage lengths. Often, manufacturers altered the original design by adding or removing frames from the fuselage. You can do the same by cutting fuselages and removing or adding sections. Some conversions involve other changes, such as trimming or extending flight surfaces and even altering the engines. A list of common conversions is found on page 45.

Measuring

The first step in changing a fuselage is to determine how much needs to be removed or added to the fuselage for the conversion. Some kits have cut marks on the inside of the fuselage, **1**.

Changes to a fuselage are usually represented by a measurement or by number of windows. That measurement has to be transferred to the model. I mark the edge of the cuts with tape, **2**. If the measurement relates to window frames, cut along edges of the openings rather than trying to get it exactly between them. When modifying a fuselage without molded windows, measure and mark the cuts with a ruler and marker, **3**. If possible, make the cuts in the areas of the fuselage having a constant diameter rather than in tapered

areas or those with wing boxes to minimize sanding and filling. If the fuselage is long enough, stagger the cuts to give the joins more stability.

Cutting

It's possible to make clean, straight cuts by hand, but using a miter box makes life a lot easier. Place the model in the miter box and align the edge of the tape with the teeth of a razor saw placed through the 90-degree slots, **4**. Begin cutting slowly, keeping an eye on the saw's progress to ensure that it doesn't stray. Be sure that the model doesn't move also. You can cut narrow bodies taped together, but wide

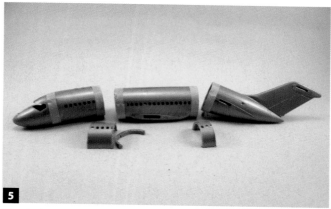

5 Here's the DC-9 after the cuts. I saved the sections because I'll use the two larger pieces to build a -50 aircraft.

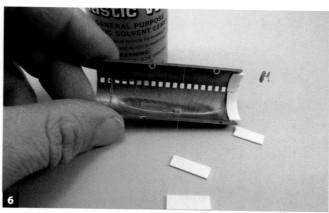

6 To improve fit and alignment between the DC-9 fuselage section, I glued strips of .030" styrene along one side of each join.

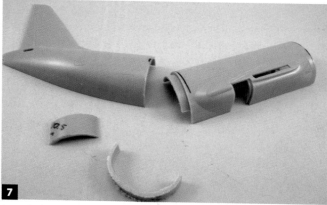

7 I used parts of the surplus fuselage sections to make alignment tabs on the 737.

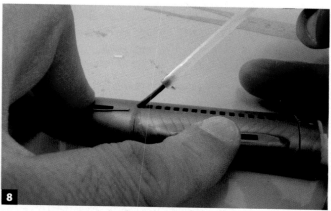

8 Placing three parts of fuselage half on glass, I pushed them together and applied glue. The glass keeps the centerline joining surface flat; a straightedge ensures the fuselage stays plumb.

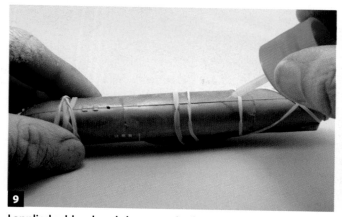

9 I applied rubber-band clamps to the fuselage to guard against warping as I glued the DC-9 fuselage together.

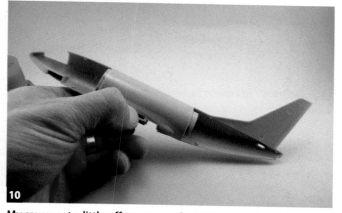

10 My saw went a little off course on the 737 conversion. To get the right alignment, I glued the better half together on glass and then added the other half one section at a time.

bodies will probably need to be cut as halves.

In a few minutes, you should be rewarded with several fuselage parts, **5**. Clean up any rough edges with sanding sticks, being careful not to sand past the tape.

Joining

While I cut narrow bodies taped together, I prefer to reassemble the fuselage in halves. Reinforce the joins by gluing strips of styrene along one side, **6**. You can also use sections of the fuselage cutout; it has the advantage of being curved so it fits well, **7**.

Push the fuselage sections together on a flat surface, such as a pane of glass, to get the correct alignment and then flow liquid cement into the gap, **8**. These joins need to dry completely before gluing the halves together, **9**.

If you aren't sure a cut edge is straight,

COMMON CONVERSIONS

These conversions are the easiest to do for the following kits. The information was collected from a variety of sources including magazines, decal sheet instructions, and websites including air-linercafe.com and the Airliner Modeling Digest discussion group at yahoo.com.

Airfix BAC 1-11-200
To -500: Add .71" (18.1mm) forward of wing and .41" (10.5mm) aft of the wing. Extend each wingtip .21" (5.3mm).

Airfix Boeing 737-200
To -100: Remove 5.2" (13.2mm) (2 windows) fore and aft of the wing.

To -200 (advanced): Replace the kit engines with BraZ resin.

Airfix Comet 4B
To 4C: Add .3" (7.6mm) to each wing and remove wing fences. Add wing tanks as required.

Airfix DC-9-30 1/144 scale
(These measurements should work for the AZ Models (Fly) DC-9-30.)
To -10: Remove .8" (20mm) ahead of the wing and .45" (11.4mm) aft. Horizontal stabilizers have no anhedral. Add wing fences to leading edges and sand off leading edge slats. Decrease chord by trimming about .078" (2mm) from the leading edge and then sand to shape.

To -40: Add .26" (6.6mm) both fore and aft of the wing.

To -50: Add .53" (13.5mm) in front of wing and .40" (10.1mm) aft. Add styrene strip strakes ahead of forward doors.

Airfix Hawker-Siddeley Trident 1C
To 1E: Extend wingtips .22" (5.5mm).

Airfix McDonnell-Douglas DC-10-30
To -10: Remove .42" (10.7mm) from each wingtip. Leave off centerline main landing gear.

Hasegawa Lockheed L-1011-1 Tristar 1/200 scale
To -500: Remove .6" (15.2mm) (6 windows) ahead of the wing and .21" (5.3mm) (2 windows) behind the wing. The aft cut will have to go around the rear end of the wing box so the center section includes the fairing. Cut out a corresponding section of the rear section to accommodate the fairing. Add extended fillet in front of the center engine. Extend each wingtip .26" (6.75mm).

Hasegawa 1/200 scale DC-9-40
To -10: Remove .76" (19.3mm) ahead of the wing and .515" (13mm) aft. Remove .18" (4.6mm) from wingtips and leading edge slats. Add leading edge fences. Horizontal stabs should have no anhedral.

To -20: Remove .76" (19.3mm) ahead of the wing and .515" (13mm) aft.

To -30: Remove .19" (4.8mm) forward and behind wing.

To -50: Add .38" (9.7mm) ahead of wing and .285" (7.2mm) aft. Add strakes forward of doors.

Minicraft 737-300
To -500: Remove .413" (10.5mm) ahead of the wing and .275" (7mm) behind it.

Minicraft 737-400
To -300: Remove .417" (10.5mm) plugs both ahead and aft of the wing.

To -500: Remove .83" (21mm) ahead of the wing and .69" (17.5mm) aft of the wing.

Minicraft 757-200
To -300: Add 1.11" (28.2mm) ahead of the wing and .637" (16.2mm) aft. Add tail skid.

Minicraft 777
To -300: Add 1.44" (36.8mm) between the second door and the wing and 1.31"

(33.3mm) between the wing and the third door. Add tail skid and extra door over wing. Alter landing gear.

Minicraft MD-80 1/144 scale
To MD-87: Remove .79" (19.9mm) ahead of the wing and .66" (16.7mm) aft of the wing. Build up the top of the fin or replace it with resin from BraZ.

Revell Germany Airbus A319
To A318: Remove .220" (5.6mm) ahead of the wing and .433" (11mm) aft of the wing (complicated by the fuselage taper and wing fairing). Extend vertical stabilizer .192" (4.9mm). Cargo doors are narrower than on the A319 so fill them and replace with decals.

Revell Germany Avro RJ85/Bae 146-200
To RJ70/-100: Remove 2 windows fore and aft of the wing.

To RJ100/-300: Add 2 windows fore and aft of the wing.

Revell or Zvezda 767-300 1/144 scale
To -200: Remove .811" (20.6mm) ahead of the wing and .929" (23.6mm) aft of the wing. Remove tail skid.

Revell Germany 737-800
To -600: Remove 1.2" (30.4mm) and 1.05" (26.8mm). Add .03" (.7mm) extension to vertical stabilizer. Remove tail skid.

To -700: Remove .74" (18.7mm) ahead of the wing and .78" (19.75mm) aft of wing. Remove tail skid.

To -900: Add .42" (10.7mm) ahead of the wing and .28" (7.1mm) aft of the wing.

Revell Germany Fokker 100
To 70: Remove .59" (15mm) forward and .58" (14.8mm) aft of the wing.

11 For comparison, here's the modified fuselage half for the DC-9-10 (top) and the original -30 kit part.

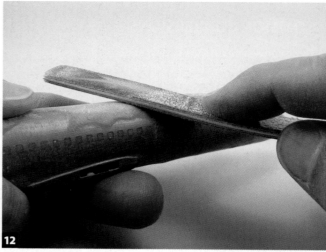

12 I filled gaps between the sections with a liberal dose of Apoxie Scuplt and sanded everything smooth. It took a few applications of super glue to eliminate all of the gaps.

13 To complete the DC-9-30 transformation to the earlier model, I had to trim the wingtips. I made the first cuts with a razor saw.

14 Then I cleaned up the cut and restored the area's aerodynamic shape with sanding sticks.

15 To reduce the DC-9's wing chord, I trimmed about 2mm from the leading edge with a saw.

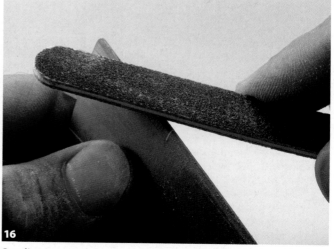

16 Sanding restored the leading-edge curve. Check your work often to avoid unevenness or flat spots.

17 To extend the wings of Airfix's Trident 1C to the span of the 1E, I first sliced off the tips and put them aside for later.

18 I made the wing graft by laminating two 5.5mm wide strips of .040" styrene. Cut the strips slightly longer than the wing chord.

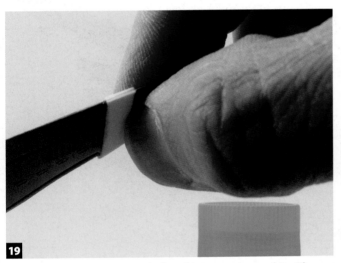

19 I used liquid cement to attach the wing extension and tip. The slow set time gave me time to adjust the fit.

20 Putty and sanding blended the graft into the wing. I scribed new panel lines and control-surface outlines.

glue one half together and then add the other half, one section at a time, **10**. Ultimately, you should have a fuselage for a whole new model, **11**.

No matter how clean your cuts are, you'll still need to fill gaps. I apply epoxy putty for the initial layer and sand it flush, **12**. Any remaining problems are usually easily handled with super glue.

Wings and things

Big changes in fuselage length often have a corresponding change in the span of wings or stabilizers.

Shortening these parts is easy. After figuring out how much needs to be removed, cut the wing with a saw, **13**. Then reshape the wingtip by sanding and

filing, **14**. If the cut is deep, you may need to fill a gap with super glue before shaping the tip.

On some conversions, the chord, the distance between the leading and trailing edges, changes. The DC-9 is a good example: in addition to a shorter fuselage, the wings of early versions of the aircraft had shorter chord and no leading-edge slats.

I marked a line about 2mm aft of the leading edge with a piece of tape. Then I cut along that line with a razor saw, **15**. You are removing a thin sliver of plastic so work slowly and deliberately to avoid mistakes. Once the cut was done, I reestablished the airfoil shape of the leading edge with a sanding stick, **16**.

To extend wings or stabilizers, you'll need to graft styrene. Converting Airfix's 1/144 scale Hawker-Siddley Trident 1C to the -1E, you need to add about 5mm to each wing.

First, I cut the tips from each wing just at the spot where the leading edge begins to curve, **17**. Use tape to keep the cut straight.

Next, I cut 5.5mm wide strips of .040" styrene and laminated two layers, producing a piece as thick as the wing, **18**.

I glued a piece slightly longer than the chord of the wing using liquid cement and then attached the tip, **19**. Repeated applications of putty and sanding blended the plug, **20**. I then restored control surfaces with scribing.

Detailing and improving kits 5

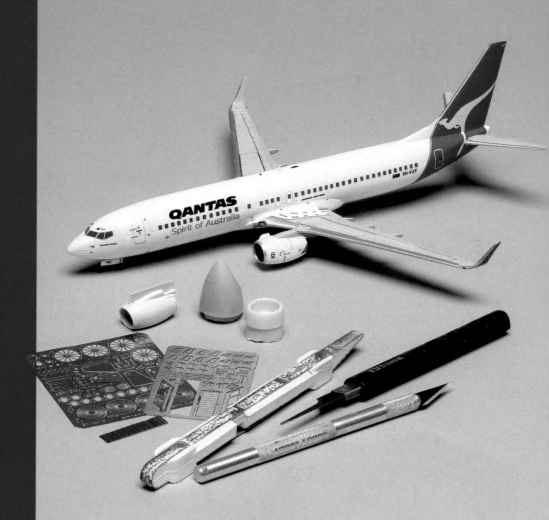

Computer design and modern molding have done wonders for plastic kits in recent years. The finesse of small parts and the level of detail seen in kits released today are light-years ahead of the clunky, sometimes crude offerings of even 30 years ago. But, as it's been said, no kit is perfect. Some come close, but all can benefit from a little extra work to add detail or correct problems. This chapter describes techniques for improving kits, by adding detail either with scratchbuilt or aftermarket parts, and those for correcting common problems. A list of solutions for fixing problems found in popular airliner kits is located on pages 64–65.

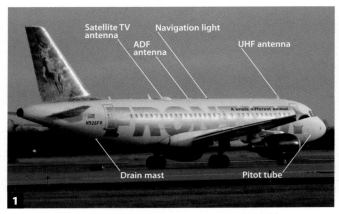

1

Airliners like this Frontier Airbus A319 are covered with antennas, lights, and other bumps.

Satellite TV antenna
ADF antenna
Navigation light
UHF antenna
Drain mast
Pitot tube
N926FR

2

When cutting thin styrene, don't cut through in one pass. Make several light passes to avoid curling or distorting the plastic.

3

Trim the front and rear edges of the antenna by pressing a knife flat against the part and pushing evenly.

4

Attach an antenna by dipping the edge in super glue and then holding it against the model.

5

I added a second ADF antenna to Revell Germany's A319 kit, using the molded one as an pattern.

6

Salami-sliced styrene rod is perfect for creating navigation lights. Glue them along the centerline on top and under the airplane.

Antennas, pitots, and drains

Next time you look at an airliner, examine the fuselage especially along the centerline, top and bottom. Commercial aircraft are festooned with small objects including radio and navigational antennas, pitot tubes (for measuring airspeed), and drain masts, **1**. Some manufacturers, like Revell Germany, mold these features onto one

fuselage half. Others, like Airfix, include them as parts to be added later or use decals to represent them. And some kits don't include them at all. Adding them is a quick way to add realism and prevent your model from looking like a toy.

The most obvious, and perhaps the easiest, parts to add are VHF communications aerials (sometimes called blade antennas).

These are the shark-fin shaped protrusions usually seen along the centerline of the fuselage top and bottom. Most airliners have several. I cut them from .010" styrene. In 1/144 scale, these antennas are 2–3mm long, so I start with a strip that wide, **2**. The leading edge of the antenna is about 30 degrees from vertical. I start the cut for the trailing edge slightly less than 1mm from

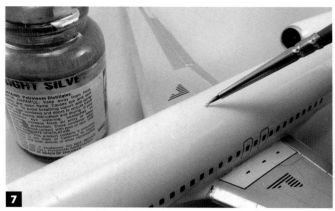

7 Paint styrene-rod lights silver and then add clear red to give them the correct appearance.

8 Transparent red plastic is a great way to model navigation lights. I stretched a bit of sprue from a car kit and then sliced off a section.

9 Start pitot tubes by super gluing styrene pieces to the airframe. After the glue sets, trim the pieces about 1mm above the surface.

10 Stretched sprue forms the tubes. Attach more than you need and then trim it to the correct length.

the front and angle the cut so the lower rear corner is directly under the upper front corner, **3**. To attach an antenna, I hold it with tweezers, touch the bottom edge to a small puddle of super glue, and then place the part on the model, **4**.

One or more oval- or teardrop-shaped automatic direction finder (ADF) antennas are usually seen along the centerline of the aircraft. To add them, cut the shapes from .010" styrene and glue them to the fuselage, **5**.

To replicate navigation lights on the fuselage, you can glue small pieces of styrene rod to the fuselage and then sand them to shape, **6**. Paint the light silver and then clear red, **7**. Alternatively, you can attach clear styrene rod or stretch clear red sprue (commonly found in automobile kits) over a candle flame, **8**, and attach that to the model.

Pitot heads are small blade objects with a bullet-shaped head usually mounted in small groups around the nose

of modern jetliners, **9**. I super glue a tiny rectangle of .010" styrene to the model, trim it to size, and then attach a short piece of stretched sprue to the top, **10**.

Drain masts, used to dump wastewater, are mounted underneath the fuselage. They are wider than the UHF antennas and end with a tube angled down and aft. I cut this shape from .010" styrene and thickened the front and bottom edges with strips of .010" styrene, **11**.

In the last decade, satellite television has become available on commercial flights. A large, round lump-shaped antenna on top of the fuselage receives this signal. I make these antennas by laminating sheet styrene together and sanding it to shape, **12**.

On a 1/144 scale narrow-body airliner, the satellite antenna will be about 10mm in diameter. You'll need to sand the lower part to conform to the fuselage, **13**. After gluing it in place, blend the attachment pedestal with putty and sanding.

Landing gear and bays

Some kits have properly shaped and well-detailed landing gear bays. Others have simple boxes, unrealistically shallow bays, or no bays at all.

You can add detail to landing gear legs or bays with fine wire and styrene stock. Examine photos to get these details right. How much you add is a matter of personal choice, but think of how visible the bays will be on the finished model. Keep in mind that on many airliners, the major bay section is often closed except when the gear is cycling, so there's little need to detail those areas.

A few aircraft—the 737 is perhaps the best-known example—don't use doors. Instead, the gear retracts to fit flush with the skin of the aircraft, so the main gear bay is visible when the aircraft is parked.

Some 737 kits (Revell Germany and Skyline) have gear bay inserts to fill the space in the belly. Minicraft's 737s don't, which leaves the interior of the fuselage

11

I reinforced the join between a drain mast and the fuselage by adding a little thin super glue with a toothpick.

12

After laminating styrene sheet, I sanded it to shape for a satellite television antenna to mount on a Frontier A319.

13

Careful dry-fitting and sanding adjusted the satellite television antenna's fit to the Airbus fuselage.

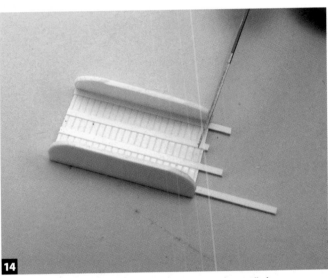

14

I built a main gear bay for Minicraft's 737 with .030" sheet styrene, HO scale siding, and styrene strip and rod.

15

The outline of Airfix's 737 nose gear bay is correct, but the depth is way too shallow, with no room for scale landing gear.

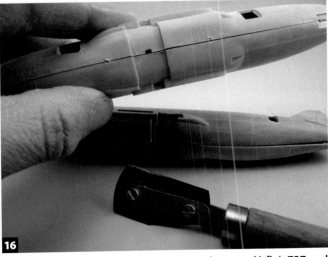

16

I cut open the shallow molded main gear bays on Airfix's 737 and then fit a styrene box similar to the one I made for Minicraft's kit.

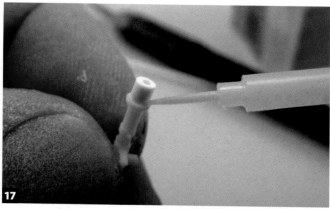

17

I extended the main gear legs of Minicraft's MD-80 by first gluing a 2mm piece of ³⁄₃₂" styrene tube over the locator pin and then gluing in a piece of .040" styrene rod to make a new locator.

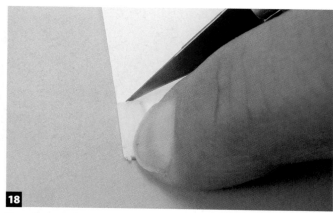

18

To make a scale thin main gear door for Minicraft's MD-80, I traced the kit part onto .010" styrene sheet with a hobby knife. Don't cut all the way through the styrene.

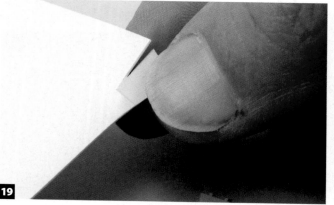

19

Grasp the part and snap it out of the styrene sheet.

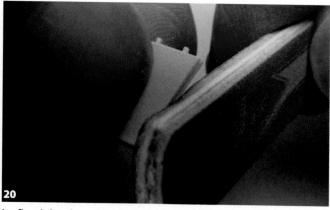

20

I refined the shape by sanding the styrene against the kit door.

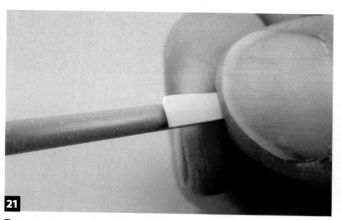

21

To curve styrene sheet for a 737 nose gear door, I bent it around a piece of sprue.

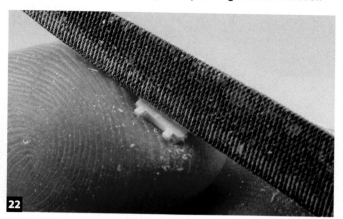

22

I thinned the kit doors of Minicraft's MD-80 by sanding the inside face with a half-round file.

visible through the open bay. I built a replacement bay from .030" styrene, used HO scale grooved styrene siding for the ceiling, and added strips of styrene to replicate stringers, **14**.

On many Airfix kits, the bays are molded as shallow depressions, barely deeper than the thickness of the plastic, **15**. If the bays are small, this might work okay, but for larger bays such as on the 737-200, the undersize bays will be obvious. Cut away the plastic lining the bay and replace it with a styrene box, **16**. Because the bay is deeper, there's a good chance you'll need to extend the landing gear leg with styrene or brass rod, **17**.

One of the easiest ways to improve the scale appearance of a small-scale airliner is replacing thick landing-gear doors with .015" sheet styrene. Place the part on the styrene and score around it with a hobby knife, **18**. Then snap the part out, **19**. Refine the shape by holding the kit part over the styrene replacement during sanding, **20**. You can bend the part against brass rod, a pen, or a piece of sprue to get the right curve, **21**.

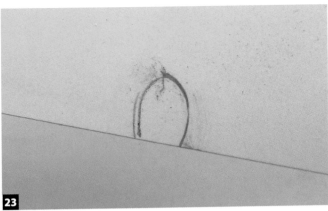

23
I drew the outline of a DC-9-10 wing fence onto .005" styrene.

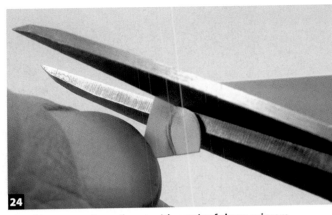

24
The thin styrene is easily cut with a pair of sharp scissors.

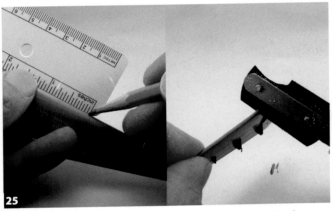

25
After marking the location of the fence on the DC-9 wing, I cut a slot with a JLC razor saw.

26
I slipped the fence into the slot on the wing and then touched a brush filled with Tamiya Extra Thin Liquid Cement to the join.

27
Looking into the intake of a Minicraft 737 engine, you can see a locator ridge rather than a smooth sleeve.

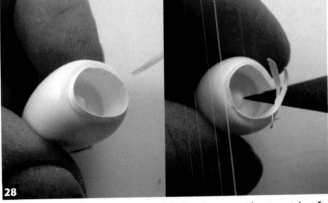

28
The engines on 737-300s are flat on the bottom. I bent a strip of .010" styrene into the opening, glued it, then trimmed the excess.

If you want to use the kit doors, you can file them thin. Use a round file to maintain curves, **22**.

Wing fences

Lots of airliners have aerodynamic structures on the wings commonly referred to as wing fences. They can be small objects wrapped around the leading edge of a wing as seen on the Boeing 727 or the Airbus A300. Or they can extend for much of the wing chord, as on the Vickers VC-10. Many kits either omit the fences or mold them in incorrect locations.

It's easy to make fences from .005" styrene, **23** and **24**. I recommend cutting them slightly oversize and then sanding them to shape on the model. Alternatively, attach smaller leading edge fences by cutting a slot in the leading edge and inserting the fence, **25** and **26**.

Engine intakes

Some kits have incorrectly shaped or incomplete intake trunks, **27**. Most jet engines feature a smooth transition from

29 To make intake sleeves, I airbrushed clear decal film with Tamiya dark sea gray acrylic and then sealed it with Microscale Liquid Decal Film.

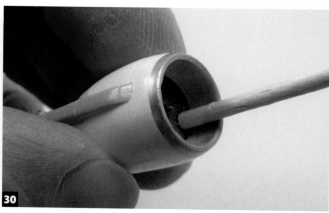

30 To get the right size for the decal, I marked the lip on a wooden skewer.

31 Slide the intake decal off the backing paper and wrap it around a metal tube or knife handle slightly smaller than the intake.

32 A stripe of a different shade of gray adds interest and realism to Revell Germany's A320 engines. Check references for the right colors and intake style.

intake ring to fan. If the model has a void or the detail is incomplete, insert styrene or brass tube. If the engine is not perfectly round, like the CFM engines in Minicraft's 737, I cut a piece of .010" styrene, trimmed it to fit inside the engine, and then glued it in place, **28**. Fill minor gaps with thin super glue or Mr. Surfacer.

Many intakes feature a noise-absorbing lining. It's possible to paint these panels, but the easiest way to make them look correct is with decals. I painted some clear decal paper with medium gray acrylic paint and then sealed it with decal film, **29**. After measuring the depth of the intake, **30**, I cut a piece wide enough to fit the intake and long enough to wrap all the way around. Take your time positioning this decal, **31**. You can divide the panels with thin strips of lighter gray decal, **32**.

Flaps and slats

Modern airliner wings are a marvel of moving parts and variable geometry

designed to allow an airplane capable of flying at Mach .9 to handle speeds as low as 120 miles per hour during take off and landing. To represent a plane taxiing, taking off, or touching down, it's necessary to reposition the leading edge slats and trailing edge flaps. Be warned that this is rarely as simple as cutting the wing along the outline of the control surface and reattaching the flap at an angle. Like an iceberg, part of the flaps are hidden inside the wing during normal flight, and some are double- or triple-slotted. This means scratchbuilding the missing portions.

First, cut the parts off the wing, either by repeatedly scoring along the seam with a knife or scriber, **33**, or using a razor saw, **34**. Save the parts, **35**. Check photos to see which parts need to be removed and how the flaps and slats work.

For single-piece flaps, graft sheet styrene onto the forward edge of the flap and sand it to an airfoil shape, **36**.

For double- or triple-slotted flaps, cut strips of styrene to fit, **37**. You'll also need to modify the flap tracks to reflect the changes, **38**.

Slats usually slide forward and down, revealing hidden sections along the leading edge, so first build the leading edge behind the slats with styrene strips, **38**. You can build slats from sheet styrene or the severed leading edges, **39**.

Reshaping parts

When modeling airliners, you'll run into incorrectly shaped kit parts. If the issue is excess plastic, it's easy to sand away the problem. Sometimes the only way to build the airliner you want is by modifying another version, which is what I had to do to build a Vickers VC-10. The only kit I could find was Airfix's RAF tanker version, which meant cutting off some lumps and bumps not seen on the airliner. The largest of these is hollow and simply cutting it off would have created a big hole in the rear fuselage.

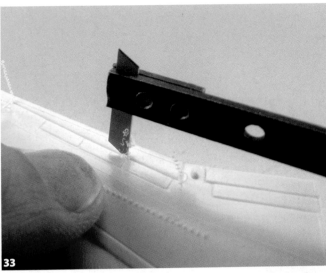

33

I began cutting out the flaps on Airfix's 1/144 scale 737 wing by scoring along the front edge with a scriber.

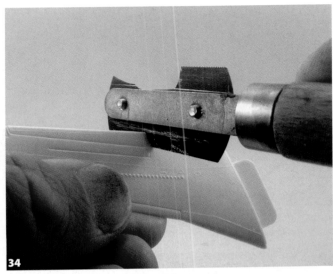

34

I cut out the sides of the flaps with a razor saw.

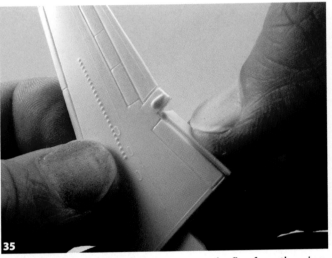

35

After scoring and cutting, it's easy to snap the flap from the wing. Set it aside for later.

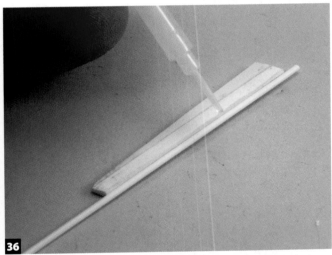

36

Styrene rod glued to the leading edge of the flap and sanded replicates the section that's buried in the wing during operation.

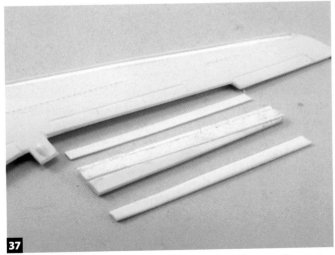

37

On airliners with slotted flaps, deploying them is more than cutting and repositioning. I added styrene strips to make extra flaps.

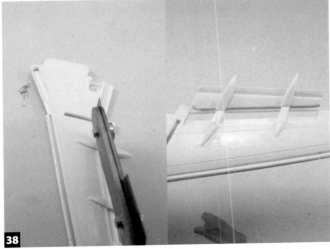

38

I cut the flap actuator fairings under the 737 wing, extended them with styrene rod, and glued the flap sections onto them.

39 After gluing styrene strip into the slat gap, I reattached the leading edge device.

40 The refueling fairing underneath the tail of Airfix's VC-10 K.2 had to go. I filled it first with Milliput epoxy putty to eliminate the void.

41 On Airfix's Airbus A300B, the tail cone has a step not seen on the airplane. I built the area up with Milliput and sanded it to shape.

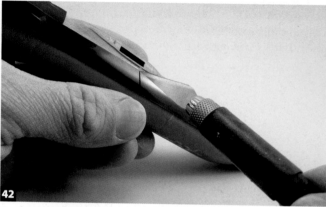

42 Dragging the back edge of a hobby knife along the tape edge will remove a sliver of plastic each time but can be hard to control.

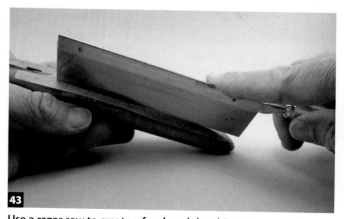

43 Use a razor saw to create a fuselage lobe chine. It's easy to keep straight and removes an even amount of plastic with each pass.

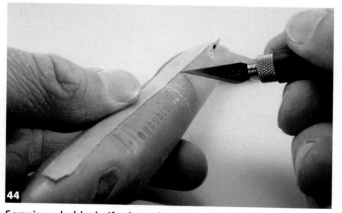

44 Scraping a hobby knife along the edge of the groove refines the shape.

Instead, I filled the bulge with epoxy putty before cutting it off, **40**. If you need to add material to a part that is too small or narrow, you can use styrene or putty, **41**.

Fuselage lobe creases

The fuselages of many airliners have upper and lower fuselage lobes usually separated on the outside by a slight chine

or indented line along the floor of the cabin. But this feature is missing on some kits like Airfix's DC-9.

Mark the chine's location with tape and then lightly cut the surface with the back of hobby knife, **42**, or a razor saw, **43**. I prefer using a razor saw because it's easier to make the cut even and straight. Don't make the cut too deep. Refine the chine

by lightly scraping, **44**, or sanding the plastic on either side, **45**.

Photoetched metal

Plastic molding technology has limitations, especially on how thin parts can be formed.

Metal is often a good replacement for too-thin plastic, and photoetched-metal

45

You can also lightly sand across the groove.

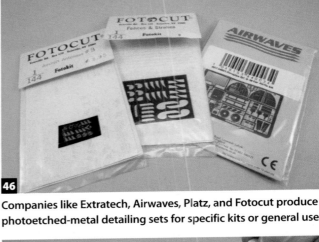

46

Companies like Extratech, Airwaves, Platz, and Fotocut produce photoetched-metal detailing sets for specific kits or general use.

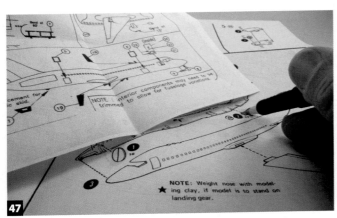

47

Photoetched-metal parts replace or modify kit parts, so I compare instruction sheets and make notes about parts to be modified.

48

I primed Airwaves photoetched-metal parts for the DC-9 while still on the fret.

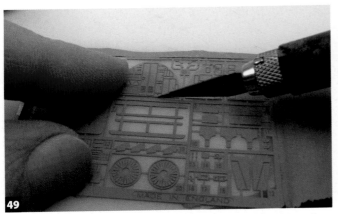

49

For clean cuts and less damage to delicate photoetched-metal parts, I use a piece of hard, smooth plastic as a cutting board.

50

Place the fret on the sticky part of a Post-it Note to avoid losing small parts during cutting.

parts have become an important option for modelers, **46**.

Photoetching involves thin sheets of brass or stainless steel covered with light-sensitive material being exposed to light through a negative-like film. The sheet is then placed in acid, which removes some of the material and leaves thin metal parts.

You'll find generic details as well as sets designed to fit a specific kit. Most include instructions showing part locations and modifications needed to fit the parts. Before starting a project involving after-market parts, I compare instructions and make notes on the sheets, **47**.

Paint doesn't always adhere well to bare metal, so I usually prime the parts

while they're still attached to the frets, **48**.

To remove parts, I place the fret on a hard surface, such as glass, and run a sharp hobby knife through the thin metal attachment points along the edge of the part, **49**. To avoid parts going airborne during cutting, try placing the fret along the sticky portion of a Post-it Note, **50**, or inside a zip-close bag, **51**.

51 You can also place the fret inside a zipper-close bag and cut through it to avoid losing any parts.

52 A sanding stick and a firm grip make quick work of the nub of metal left from the attachment point.

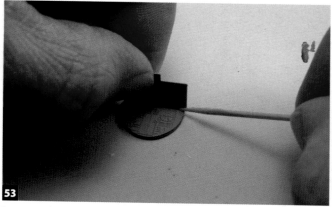

53 I ran super glue into the join between the interior parts from the Airwaves DC-9 set with a wooden toothpick.

54 You can use a pair of razor blades to bend photoetched metal. Use one as the folding edge and the other to lever the part up.

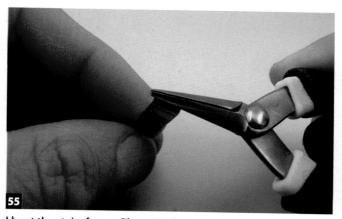

55 I bent the stairs from a Platz 727 detail set using a pair of smooth-jawed pliers from Tamiya.

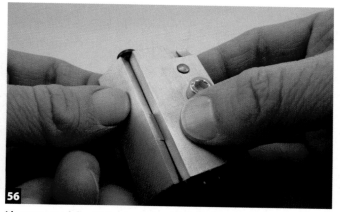

56 I bent part of the 727 set using a 3D Detail Tools elbow bender from UMM-USA.

Eliminate the attachment point by running a sanding stick or file along the part's edge. **52**. Use super glue to join photoetched parts or attach them to plastic, **53**. Some parts need to be bent to shape before gluing. You can achieve simple bends with two razor blades, **54**, a pair of tweezers, or pliers, **55**. If you need to do complex bends, consider acquiring a bending tool such as the Hold & Fold, the Mission Models Etch Mate, or a 3D Detail Tools bender, **56**. These tools clamp one part securely and provide a solid straight edge to bend the metal against.

Resin

Resin has become an increasingly important ingredient of modeling over the last 15–20 years. In addition to aftermarket parts, whole airliner kits are frequently cast in resin. Resin can hold a sharp edge better than plastic, so these parts provide a level of detail not usually possible with kit parts. Resin parts need to be handled slightly differently than plastic ones, but they are generally as easy to handle.

57

Soak resin engines and winglets overnight in Westley's Bleche-Wite to remove mold-release agent.

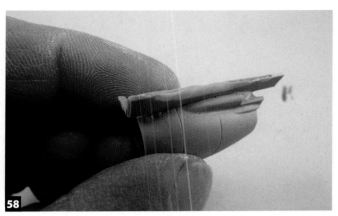

58

The pour plug on Contrail's 737NG engines runs along the top where the pylon meets the cowl.

59

I used a razor saw to carefully remove the pour plug from the front of the 737 engine hot section.

60

I applied super glue with a toothpick to fill pinholes and other blemishes in the resin of the Contrail engine.

61

The rear lip of the cowl on the Contrail 737 engine arrived slightly out of round.

62

I dipped the resin engine in hot water and bent it to shape, holding the engine in cold water as it cooled.

Preparation is a big part of working with resin. Before doing anything else, soak the parts overnight in a cleaner like Westley's Bleche-Wite to remove any mold-release agent left from the casting process, **57**. Although it won't harm the resin, Westley's is corrosive so wear gloves and eye protection.

Resin parts usually have excess resin—pour plugs—attached to them where the liquid resin was poured into the mold, **58**. Most can be removed with a knife or saw, **59**. Clean up the attachment points with sanding and fill any pinholes or other blemishes with super glue, **60**.

Resin parts can bend or warp during transit or handling, **61**. Hold the part in hot (not boiling) water for 30 seconds, reshape it, then dip it in cold water, **62**.

Always dry-fit resin parts and make any adjustments before committing glue to the join, **63**. Attach parts with super glue, **64**, or 5-minute epoxy, **65**.

Casting resin parts

As you build airliners, you'll probably discover that there are scratchbuilt or modi-fied parts you'll want to use more than

63 I had to trim more away from the pour plug of Contrails' 707 cockpit insert after dry-fitting showed that it didn't fit.

64 Thin super glue flowed into the gap joined Contrails' resin winglet to Revell's 737 wing.

65 I used 5-minute epoxy to secure a resin cockpit insert to Minicraft's 707 fuselage. The longer working time allows adjustments.

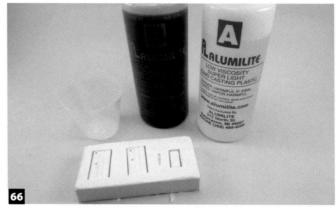

66 A resin-casting set like this one from Alumilite contains everything you need to get started making your own parts.

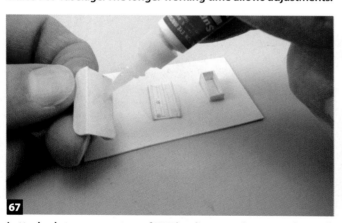

67 I attached styrene masters of 737 landing gear bays to a sheet of styrene with super glue.

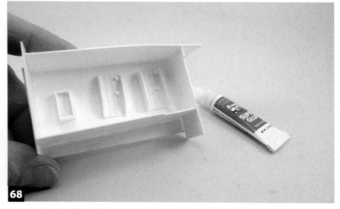

68 I attached walls of styrene glued around the masters to complete the mold.

once. Casting copies in resin is the perfect way to reproduce them.

You can buy casting supplies separately, but a first-time caster may find it easiest to invest in a starter set such as those sold by Alumilite, **66**.

After creating a master, attach it to a sheet of styrene with super glue, **67**. Then build walls for the mold with styrene, leaving at least ½" between the parts and the walls, **68**. Lego plastic building blocks and others also work well.

The walls need to be taller than the parts by at least ½" so the rubber or silicone mold material covers the parts but doesn't flow over the sides. Most sets include modeling clay that you can press around the mold to ensure a solid seal.

Room-temperature vulcanizing rubber comes as two parts that must be mixed. Make sure you mix them thoroughly or the mold may not set up properly, **69**.

Pour the thick liquid slowly into the mold, ensuring that it covers the parts, **70**.

Lightly tapping the mold during or after pouring helps dislodge air that can create bubbles in the mold.

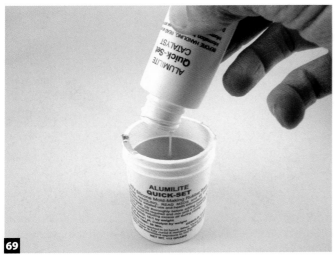

69 Mix both parts of the mold-making material thoroughly to ensure proper consistency and results.

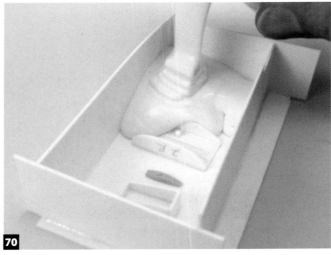

70 RTV rubber has a consistency like cake mix. Pour it into the mold from a corner to ensure complete coverage.

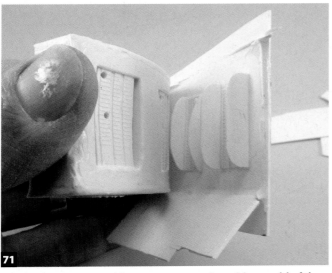

71 I broke the styrene mold apart to extract the rubber mold of the 737 bays.

72 I used a smooth-sided mixing cup to measure and mix the resin components.

73 Pour the resin quickly but smoothly into the mold to make sure it fills all the spaces before the material sets.

74 You only have a few minutes to work with the resin, or you'll end up with a solid mass in the cup and a partially filled mold.

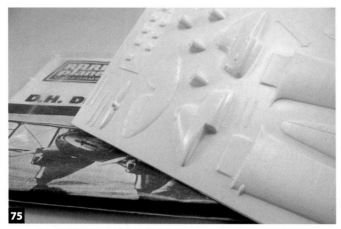

75

Rareplane's vacuum-formed Dragon Rapide comes on two sheets of parts, one in white and the other clear.

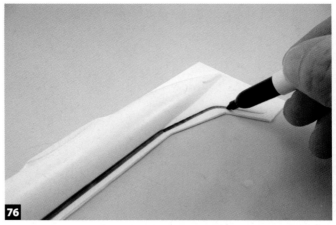

76

I traced the outline of Welsh Models' vacuum-formed Lockheed L-188 Electra with a permanent marker.

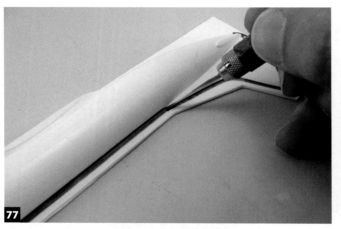

77

To remove the excess plastic, I scored around the Electra fuselage using a hobby knife held at 45 degrees for the centerline.

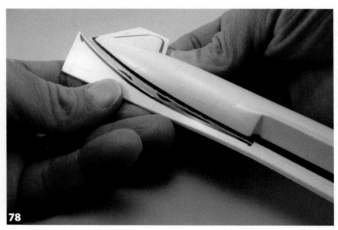

78

I snapped the fuselage away from the plastic.

Set the mold aside for several hours; check the directions because setting times can differ from rubber to rubber.

You may have to disassemble the form to get the mold out, **71**. The rubber is sturdy enough to withstand some handling, but it is possible to tear the material so take care.

Like the rubber, resin comes in two parts that need to be mixed together thoroughly.

Measure the stated amounts into a smooth-sided container and stir until the color is consistent, **72**.

Scrape the sides and corners to ensure everything is mixed.

Pour the resin into the mold, **73**, working smoothly but quickly: most resin begins to set in a few minutes, **74**.

After a few minutes, you should be able to flex the mold and remove a perfect resin copy of the original part or parts ready to be attached.

Vacuum-formed parts

Produced on a one-piece mold over which heated sheet styrene is drawn by air pressure, vacuum-form (or vacform) kits and parts used to be a mainstay of modeling. They are less common now, but there are several companies, notably Welsh Models, that still produce airliner kits and conversions using this method. So it's good to know how to build vacuum-formed models.

The first thing you'll notice about these kits is that the parts, rather than being attached to spruces are molded into large sheets of styrene, **75**. Freeing the parts from the styrene without damaging them is the critical first step in construction.

Trace the parts with a permanent marker, **76**. Press the tip into the corner of the styrene and the part so ink is transferred to both sides. Score along the border by running the tip of a No. 11 blade backwards along the corner holding

the blade at 45 degrees, **77**. After several passes, you should be able to gently snap the excess plastic away from the part, **78**. You will see a thin strip of plastic beneath the marker line, **79**. Tape a sheet of wet-dry sandpaper to a piece of glass. Place the part cut edge down on the paper and move it in a circle to remove the excess plastic, **80**. Maintain constant, gentle pressure on the part; pressing too hard will cause the part to wear unevenly. You'll know you're done when there is no white plastic below the marker, **81**.

Before gluing parts together, be sure there's nothing else you need to do such as opening landing gear holes, **82**. To reinforce long bonds and provide additional gluing surface, I attach short pieces of sheet styrene along the seam edge on one half, **83**. If I have any doubts about the strength of a seam, I pour 5-minute epoxy into the assembly and turn it so the glue runs along the inside of the seam, **84**.

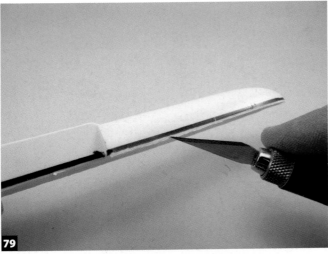

79

This picture shows the black line and the lip of styrene to be removed before the fuselage halves can be joined.

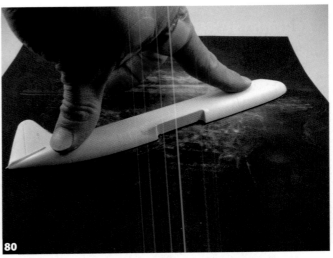

80

I pressed the Electra fuselage gently onto sandpaper taped to glass to remove the excess plastic.

81

Here's the Electra fuselage with the plastic lip sanded off.

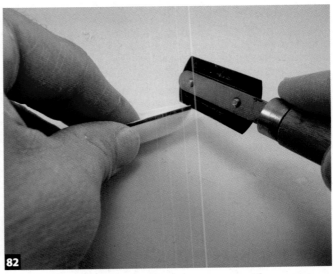

82

I cut out the opening for the Electra's nose gear with a razor saw.

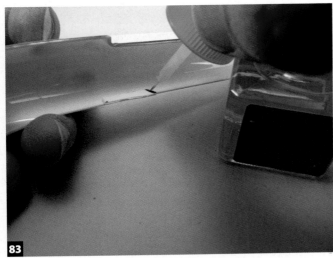

83

Before joining the fuselage halves, I glued styrene strips along one edge to aid alignment and reinforce the seam.

84

I cut open the Electra fuselage at the wing join and poured 5-minute epoxy along the fuselage seam.

ACCURIZING COMMON INJECTION-MOLDED AIRLINER KITS

This list is compiled from my own assessments where I have experience with the kits as well as from print and online kit reviews and builds. It is by no means comprehensive or exhaustive, but it should provide some hints to improving the kits.

Airfix 1/144 scale Airbus A300B2

- Front doors should be curved. The easy fix is gluing the parts in place, filling the outlines, and adding decals.
- Check references as some aircraft had Pratt & Whitney engines instead of the GEs in the kit.
- Reshape tail cone to remove step-behind rudder.
- Add leading-edge wing fences about two-thirds of the way to the tip.

Airfix 1/144 scale BAC 1-11

- Nose is blunt; add putty and sand it to more of a point.
- Add APU exhaust at tail cone using styrene tube.
- Wing fence is molded too far outboard; move it or replace it with sheet styrene.
- Remove tail bumper.

Airfix 1/144 scale Boeing 737

- Cut out and box in main gear well.
- Engines are correct for early -200 series aircraft. Need to replace them to build advanced version.

Airfix 1/144 scale Boeing 727

- Nose is too fat both left to right and top to bottom. Sand it narrower.
- Minimize center engine crease on vertical tail.
- Remove wing fence from trailing edge. Add identical shape fence to leading edge.
- Extend Kruger flap inboard to wing/fuselage join.
- Fill the bottom engraved rudder hinge.

Airfix 1/144 scale de Havilland Comet 4C

- Drill small holes between the engines.
- Relocate wing fences to just outside second wing panel line from center.

Airfix 1/144 scale Hawker-Siddeley Trident 1C

- Add wing to fuselage fillet. The port-side fairing is much shorter than the starboard to accommodate the cargo door.
- Relocate the nose gear to the port edge of the gear bay. The Trident's nose gear is off center.
- Increase dihedral to outer third of wing.

Airfix 1/144 scale Lockheed L-1011

- Reshape nose to better reflect Tristar's shape.

Airfix 1/144 scale McDonnell-Douglas DC-9

- Add lobe crease

Airfix 1/144 scale McDonnell-Douglas DC-10

- Cabin windows are too low; fill them and use decals.
- Engines hang too low. Remove extension molded on wing and part of the top of the pylon.

Airfix 1/144 scale SUD Caravelle I

- Fill cabin doors and add decals.
- Engine pylons are too wide. Remove the pylon molded on the fuselage and then sand the pylon on engines to fit fuselage.

Airfix 1/144 scale Vickers VC-10

- Remove wing root molded on the fuselage to correct wingspan by sanding the area flush with the wing box.
- Check references for correct wing fence arrangements and add them with sheet styrene.
- Fill gaps between engines; can be done by adding intake sleeves.

Doyusha 1/144 scale Boeing 777

- Fill incorrectly positioned cabin windows and windscreen, replace with decals.
- Tail cone should be reshaped to 777's vertical wedge.

Minicraft 1/144 scale Boeing 377 Stratocruiser

- There is no engine detail in the cowls, so painting or scratchbuilding will be necessary to hint at power plants.

Minicraft 1/144 scale Boeing 727-200

- Add reverser hinge housing to engines.
- Reshape wing box: it is indistinct, especially at the rear.
- Wing leading edges should be thinned.

Minicraft 1/144 scale 737-300

- Box in main wheel well.
- Add strakes to engine nacelles and intake ducting.

Minicraft 1/144 scale Boeing 737-400

- Box in main wheel well.
- Add intake ducting and engine strakes.
- Add tail skid.

Minicraft 1/144 scale Boeing 757

- Nose needs to be reshaped.
- Reshape vertical stabilizer.
- Refine fit of wings as they can sit a little cockeyed to the fuselage centerline.
- Engines hang at an odd angle: file pylons to adjust attitude.
- Shim landing gear so aircraft sits level.

Minicraft 1/144 scale Douglas DC-3

- Sand down too-tall vertical tail.
- Build up fuselage above cockpit with putty.
- Make main wheels fatter.

Minicraft 1/144 scale Lockheed L-188 Electra

- Fuselage is incorrectly shaped, especially around nose and tail: will require extensive reshaping or replacement with Welsh vacuum-formed fuselage.

Minicraft 1/144 scale MD-80

- Extend rear gear legs .078" (2mm) to correct stance.

Revell Germany 1/144 scale 737-800

- Windows are molded .078" (2mm) too low on fuselage. Fill them and use decals. You'll need to fill and rescribe panel lines along window strip.
- Engine intake lips are a little too flat on bottom. Modify them with styrene or replace them with aftermarket engines.

Revell 1/144 scale 747-400

- Nose narrows too soon. It needs to be fattened along window line.
- Windshield is mounted too high; fill, sand, and reshape the area.
- Wing angle of attack is too extreme. Locator slots have to be opened up so leading edge can be rotated down.

Revell 1/144 scale 767-300

- Kit engines roughly resemble Pratt & Whitney JT9Ds used on some 767s. Modify intake lip, cone, and pylon rear to model GE engine.

Zvezda 1/144 scale 767-300

- Molded door and window arrangement is correct for one version of the -300. Fill windows and doors, and use decals to represent the version you are modeling.

Weathering

More than just the effect of atmospheric conditions, weathering is a collection of finishing techniques designed to add realism to a model as well as simulate wear and tear. At first blush, it may seem strange to talk about airliners and weathering together. Finished in glossy colors, airliners are flying billboards for an airline and are kept clean, right? Well, sort of.

23

Rain leaves faint streaks below the cabin windows. I brushed these marks on the MD-82 with light gray pastels.

24

Jet bridges leave a faint square around the cabin door. I painted this on with light gray pastels.

25

I followed panel lines around the engines and rear fuselage to turn this SAS MD-82 into a well-used passenger carrier.

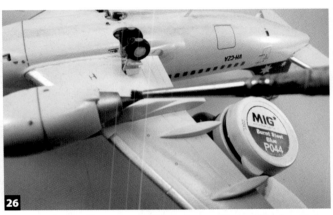

26

To hint at heat-affected metal, I brush metallic and black pastels around a jet engine's hot section.

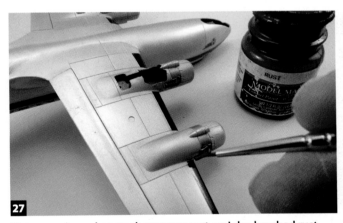

27

Piston-engine exhausts show some rust, so I dry-brushed rust over gunmetal to create the right look on Minicraft's C-54.

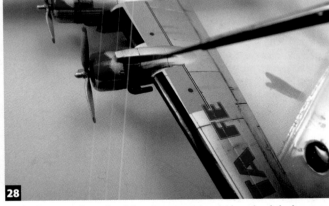

28

Oil leaks, even from healthy piston engines. I brushed dark gray pastels behind the cowls of Minicraft's C-54.

them a dark rust red-brown, **27**. Don't make them too bright.

Add exhaust staining aft of the pipes in the direction of airflow. Piston engines are notorious for oil leaks—the joke is "If you're not leaking oil, you're in trouble because the engine is dry."—so I add a few oil streaks behind the cowl flaps, **28**. Make sure not to overdo these

unless you are modeling a high-hour cargo plane.

Don't handle the model any more than necessary after applying pastels because they'll come off on your fingers and leave fingerprints. Some modelers seal pastels under a clear coat, but this tends to alter the color or tone. I prefer to leave them alone and handle the model

by an unweathered wingtip or attach it to a base.

How much is too much?

I use photos of the actual airliner I am modeling as a guide. Generally, if I look at the model and think it may need just a little more, I stop. Subtlety is the key to a realistic finish.

7

I've been inspired by the work of talented modelers from around the world. Here's a small sample, and each modeler shares a little about how they built and painted the model. I have also included a few of my models.

Empire Air DC-3
Modeler: Tim Bradley, Seattle, Washington
Scale: 1/72
Kit: Italeri (Revell)
Decals: Hand-made
Paint: Alclad II metallic sealed with Future

Tim added oil lines to engines, wire antennas, Mosskit exhausts, MV Products lenses for landing lights, and a few photoetched-metal parts. "I researched and designed the decals after a 1945-50 operator based in Boise, Idaho," he said. "Trying something new, I didn't want black side window decals, so I made windows with curtains and seats."

Lufthansa 737-100
Modeler: Bill Engar, Kaysville, Utah
Scale: 1/144
Kit: Airfix
Decals: Livery: modified from Airfix 727 kit; Windows: ATP
Paint: White: Testors gloss white enamel thinned with lacquer thinner to consistency of milk; Natural metal: SnJ Spray Metal

To build one of the first 737s delivered to Luthansa, Bill removed ¼" sections from in front and behind the wing of Airfix's 737. He shortened the engines by removing ¼" and then built new exhausts from styrene tube. Bill loves the Airfix 737: "It is a great canvas for a number of interesting airline color schemes, both new and old. If I had to be stranded on a desert island with just one case of models, that's the kit I'd pick, assuming that the desert island had sources for paint, decals, and electricity!"

Hawaiian Airlines Boeing 767-300

Modeler: Juha Stenberg, Helsinki, Finland
Scale: 1/144
Kit: Revell
Decals: Flying Colors (No. FC44-039) for livery; Skyline 767 sheet (No. SKY144-50) supplied some details
Paint: White: automotive 1k lacquer; Wing light gray and dark gray on the wings: Xtracolor enamels; Leading edges and engine intakes and core: Alclad II; Fan discs: Model Master Metalizers

The model was finished with automotive 2k gloss clear coat with a small amount of matte paste added to reduce sheen slightly. A Badger 150 airbrush was used for painting.

Juha added K&S brass tube inside the intakes for a smooth appearance, and scratchbuilt antennas, angle-of-attack vanes, and pitot tubes. "I built this aircraft since I think Hawaiian has one of the most attractive liveries around," he said.

Air Jamaica Airbus A340-300

Modeler: Walt Fink, Woodstock, Illinois
Scale: 1/144
Kit: Revell Germany
Decals: Aviagraphics
Paint: White, colors, grays: Gunze Sangyo acrylics; Metallics: Testors Model Master Metalizers

Walt built the model straight out of the box. He planned to use two sets of Aviagraphics A310 decals to produce the livery but wasn't happy with the decals so the stripes are painted using Radio Shack vinyl electrical tape for masking.

Ethiopian Airlines Boeing 777-200LR

Modeler: Brad Shinn, Hatfield, Pennsylvania
Scale: 1/144
Kit: Minicraft
Decals: TwoSix (No. 144-494)

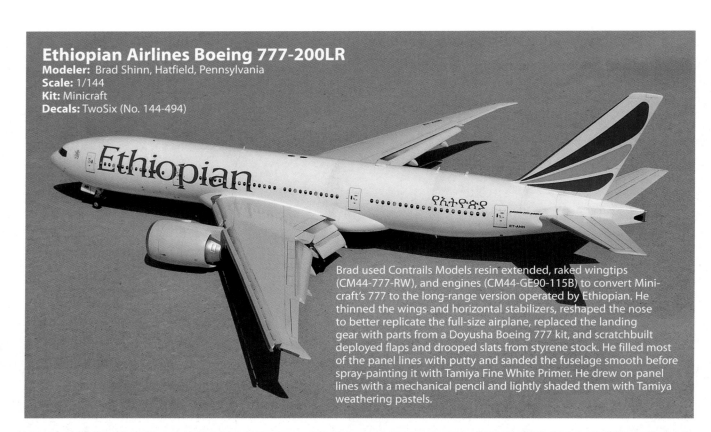

Brad used Contrails Models resin extended, raked wingtips (CM44-777-RW), and engines (CM44-GE90-115B) to convert Minicraft's 777 to the long-range version operated by Ethiopian. He thinned the wings and horizontal stabilizers, reshaped the nose to better replicate the full-size airplane, replaced the landing gear with parts from a Doyusha Boeing 777 kit, and scratchbuilt deployed flaps and drooped slats from styrene stock. He filled most of the panel lines with putty and sanded the fuselage smooth before spray-painting it with Tamiya Fine White Primer. He drew on panel lines with a mechanical pencil and lightly shaded them with Tamiya weathering pastels.

Aeroflot Tupolev Tu-114

Modeler: Jeff Thomsen, Santa Barbara, California
Scale: 1/144
Kit: Revell/Welsh
Decals: Welsh

This is a kitbash of the Revell Tu-95 bomber kit and the Welsh vacuum-formed Tu-114. "I liked the Revell kit's landing gear, props, and wings, so I grafted the vacuum-formed fuselage and tail onto it," Jeff said. The clear, plastic nose was stretch-formed over a wooden form to make it more realistic, but the rest of the windows were painted on. He rebuilt the nose gear strut using kit parts and brass wire. "I have always been fascinated by these big Russian propjets," Jeff said.

American Airlines Douglas DC-6B

Modeler: Cameron Lynch, Lakewood, Colorado
Scale: 1/144
Kit: Minicraft
Decals: Liveries Unlimited
Paint: Alclad II highly polished aluminum

Cameron replaced the engines with resin from Dana Kopher, and the props and hubs from Flying Fish Models. He primed the model with Mr. Surfacer 1000, polished that out, and airbrushed Tamiya light gray around the engines. After masking with Tamiya tape, he sprayed on metallic lacquer.

United Airlines 737-300

Modeler: Carl Knable, Wheaton, Illinois
Scale: 1/144
Kit: Minicraft
Decals: Unreleased Minicraft
Paint: Primer: Gray automotive lacquer primer; White: Duplicolor lacquer

Carl added Mylar film from old floppy disks to form seamless intakes and decorated the model with decals from a never released Minicraft kit. The stand is a circular piece of clear styrene with a piece of ⅛" polycarbonate rod glued in and inserted into a hole in the belly of the plane.

Midway Airlines CRJ

Modeler: Ben Brown, Apex, North Carolina
Scale: 1/144
Kit: Revell Germany/Welsh
Decals: A mix of homemade and Nazca
Paint: White: Tamiya white primer; Yellow: Testors enamel (square bottle);
Blue: Xtracolor insignia blue

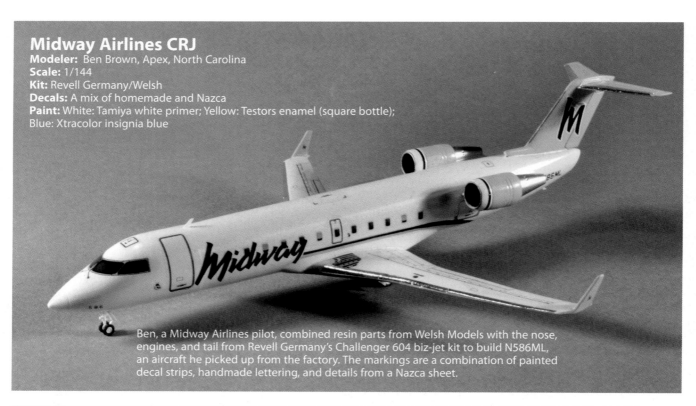

Ben, a Midway Airlines pilot, combined resin parts from Welsh Models with the nose, engines, and tail from Revell Germany's Challenger 604 biz-jet kit to build N586ML, an aircraft he picked up from the factory. The markings are a combination of painted decal strips, handmade lettering, and details from a Nazca sheet.

New York Air DC-9

Modeler: Jeffrey J. Schmitz, Spring, Texas
Scale: 1/144
Kit: Airfix
Decals: ATP
Paint: Primer, wing center sections: Floquil; Natural metal: Alclad II aluminum;
Red: Model Masters Chrysler engine red lacquer; Gloss: Pledge Future floor polish
Details: Tamiya chrome silver and black and Floquil weathered black

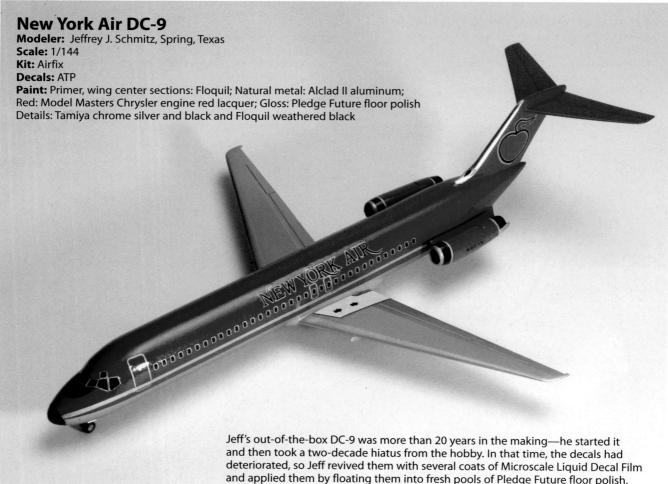

Jeff's out-of-the-box DC-9 was more than 20 years in the making—he started it and then took a two-decade hiatus from the hobby. In that time, the decals had deteriorated, so Jeff revived them with several coats of Microscale Liquid Decal Film and applied them by floating them into fresh pools of Pledge Future floor polish.

Chicago Express Saab 340

Modeler: Frank Cuden, Albert Lea, Minnesota
Scale: 1/144
Kit: Welsh
Decals: Draw
Paint: Primer: Floquil mixed with lacquer thinner; White: Testors gloss white (No. 1145); Blue: Testors dark blue (No. 1111)

The Welsh Saab is a multimedia kit with vacuum-formed fuselage, injection-molded wings and tail, and white-metal props and landing gear. Frank added styrene tube exhausts, replaced the intakes with styrene, and bolstered the detail of the landing gear with styrene rod. He even scratchbuilt windshield wipers from stretched sprue! To highlight panel lines, Frank lightly drew a soft pencil along the crease.

Alitalia Express Embraer 170-100LR

Modeler: Massimo Santarossa, Calgary, Alberta, Canada
Scale: 1/144
Kit: Hasegawa
Decals: TwoSix (No. STS44132)
Paint: Testors Model Master enamels and Alclad II metallics

Massimo built the kit straight from the box and described it as one of the most fun builds he has done. "Each time I sat down at the model bench, I came away with a smile on my face; the ease of construction was so good," he said. "I've always thought the Alitalia livery had a classic yet modern look to it."

SkyEurope 737-500
Scale: 1/144
Kit: Minicraft
Decals: BOA Agency
Paint: White: Tamiya fine surface primer; Blue: Tamiya spray can lacquer; Gray: Testors Model Master Canadian Voodoo gray

I sectioned Minicraft's 737-300 to make the shorter -500. BOA Agency decals mark it for Slovakian carrier SkyEurope.

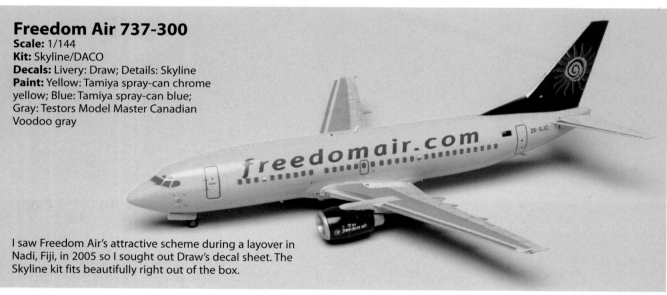

Freedom Air 737-300
Scale: 1/144
Kit: Skyline/DACO
Decals: Livery: Draw; Details: Skyline
Paint: Yellow: Tamiya spray-can chrome yellow; Blue: Tamiya spray-can blue; Gray: Testors Model Master Canadian Voodoo gray

I saw Freedom Air's attractive scheme during a layover in Nadi, Fiji, in 2005 so I sought out Draw's decal sheet. The Skyline kit fits beautifully right out of the box.

Trans World Airlines DC-9-14
Scale: 1/144
Kit: Airfix
Decals: Draw
Paint: White: Tamiya fine surface primer; Natural metal: Floquil old silver enamel and Hawkeye Hobbies SnJ aluminum

I converted Airfix's Douglas DC-9-30 to the short -14 to model one of the first short-haul jets delivered to TWA in the 1960s. In addition to chopping the fuselage, I trimmed the wings.

Imperial Japanese Airways Kawanishi H6K5-L
Scale: 1/144
Kit: Trumpeter
Decals: Kit
Paint: Natural metal: Hawkeye Hobbies Talon acrylics aluminum with polishing powder; Red: Tamiya acrylic red

One of the more unusual airliners in my collection is this Kawanishi *Mavis* flying boat. I built Trumpeter's kit out of the box.

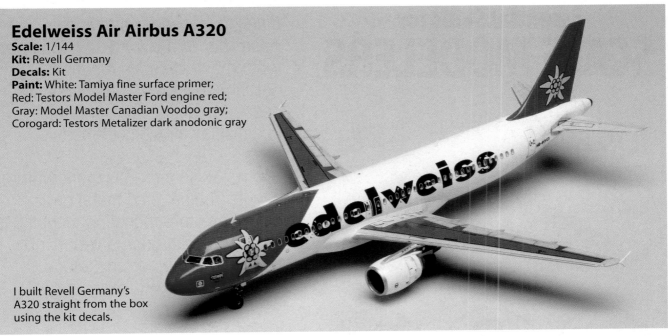

Edelweiss Air Airbus A320
Scale: 1/144
Kit: Revell Germany
Decals: Kit
Paint: White: Tamiya fine surface primer; Red: Testors Model Master Ford engine red; Gray: Model Master Canadian Voodoo gray; Corogard: Testors Metalizer dark anodonic gray

I built Revell Germany's A320 straight from the box using the kit decals.

Aaron traces his fascination with commercial aircraft to the many weekends he spent with his dad watching aircraft come and go from Brisbane, Australia's, Eagle Farm Airport. Armed with a camera, he peered through a chain-link fence as Ansett and Trans Australian Airlines 727s and DC-9s—still among his favorite airliners—touched down and climbed out. Even today, he makes time to visit his local airport and, although the smoky hot rods of the 1970s have been replaced by more modern aircraft, he still gets a thrill watching and photographing these hardworking machines. That's why he models airliners.

Aaron builds a lot of other subjects including Australian and British military aircraft, Russian and Soviet armor, and science fiction craft. Before becoming an associate editor at *FineScale Modeler*—his dream job, he says—he worked as a photographer for newspapers in Texas and Arkansas. He lives in West Allis, Wis., with his wife, Bethany, who grudgingly puts up with his impromptu trips to the airport.